Steam around London

MICHAEL WELCH

Capital Transport

ISBN 978 1 85414 449 2

Published by
Capital Transport Publishing Ltd
www.capitaltransport.com

Printed in the EU

Front cover: A train from Liverpool Street to Enfield Town enters Bethnal Green station on a sunny 7th October 1958: Class N7 No.69665 is in charge. Passengers could have been forgiven for thinking their engine had been prepared for working a Royal train. The gleaming locomotive had been scoured to perfection with burnished brass and copper fittings, bright red coupling rods and even the buffers had received some attention: well done Stratford shed. Note the station's colourful flower display and neatly whitewashed surround. On the left of the shot the tracks leading to Bishopsgate goods depot can be seen, these ceasing to be used by regular passenger trains from 1st November 1875; the substantial gradient down to Liverpool Street is clearly visible.
R.C.Riley

Title page: Stratford shed was famed for the sparkling condition of its locomotives, or at least some of them, because BR Standard 'Britannia' Pacific No.70037 *Hereward the Wake* was clearly not the shedmaster's favourite. It is seen here in absolutely dreadful external condition leaving dark and dingy Liverpool Street station in the late 1950s.
Ken Wightman

Back cover: The four chimneys of Battersea power station leave one in no doubt regarding the location of this photograph. Maunsell 'Schools' 4-4-0 No.30908 *Westminster* heads past Factory Junction with a down express on 23rd August 1958. Note that the first three vehicles represent three different eras of carriage construction, namely Maunsell, Bulleid and BR Standard. What greater variety could one wish for?
R.C.Riley

Introduction

Most people would agree that the coronation of HM the Queen (1953), the first moon landing (1969) and the fall of the Berlin wall (1989) are among the most important events in recent history, but for many steam locomotive aficionados the year 1967 probably has far more significance. At around 5.45pm on 9th July Bulleid 'Merchant Navy' Pacific No.35030 *Elder Dempster Lines* came round the curve into Waterloo station at the head of the 2.07pm from Weymouth and, after the coaches had been removed, the locomotive unceremoniously reversed out of the station to Nine Elms shed to join the long, lifeless lines of redundant motive power. That was the very last BR steam working in London and after 130 years steam traction had been forced into retirement – truly the end of an era.

London's unrivalled position as Great Britain's Capital city and largest conurbation ensured it was the focal point of the nation's railway system and most of the main trunk routes fanned out from the capital. Many of the early railway companies strove to have their own terminal in London which gave them prestige and status and, of course, the chance to benefit from rapidly increasing traffic. The first railway in the capital opened between Spa Road and Deptford on 8th February 1836 and on 14th December London's first terminal station was brought into use at London Bridge. The first train on the London & Birmingham Railway left Euston for Boxmoor on 20th July 1837 and just over a year later regular services to Birmingham commenced. A magnificent portico was erected at Euston, the station also boasting the impressive Great Hall, famous for the breadth of its unsupported ceiling. Paddington station despatched its first train, as far as Maidenhead, on 4th June 1838 while King's Cross was a relative latecomer on the scene, opening on 14th October 1852. The original Waterloo station was opened on 11th July 1848 when the existing line was extended to a site beside Waterloo bridge but the station's later development was haphazard and it became a confusing labyrinth of buildings and passageways. In 1899 powers were obtained for what was, in effect, a new station and some work was finished by the start of the First World War. That delayed completion until 1922 and the new layout, incorporating a spacious concourse, won many plaudits.

The mighty Midland Railway (MR) arrived in the capital in the mid-1860s and St Pancras station's splendid 100 feet-high and 240 feet-wide trainshed was immediately heralded as an architectural masterpiece. The MR also wanted a frontage that would have an immediate impact and commissioned Sir George Gilbert Scott, the foremost British architect of his day, to design a hotel in the Gothic Revival style. This sumptuous edifice, 'The Midland Grand Hotel', widely acknowledged to be one of the capital's most impressive buildings, was completed in 1876. Passengers to and from the eastern counties were obliged to use the inconveniently sited terminus at Bishopsgate for some years but in 1862 the Great Eastern Railway (GER), which was keen to develop commuter traffic, decided on a new terminus much closer to the city. Liverpool Street station came into use on 1st November 1875, from which date Bishopsgate was closed to passengers, and a further eight platforms were added in 1894. Victoria is essentially two distinct stations side-by-side and was largely built on the site

Contents

of a former canal basin, the 'Brighton' side dating from 1860; that part of the premises was rebuilt in 1908 with an impressive frontage. The London Chatham & Dover Railway arrived at Victoria in 1862 and, remarkably, shared their side of Victoria with the Great Western Railway which operated a service of broad gauge trains to Southall via the West London Extension. Broad gauge was soon abandoned, however, and the service ceased from 22nd March 1915.

During the late 1950s and 1960s I lived at Worthing on the Sussex coast where the vast majority of services were formed of unexciting electric units, so a trip up to London was something to be viewed with eager anticipation. The lack of security at that time at such a huge installation as Stratford motive power depot was amazing and I vaguely remember gaining entry via the Low Level platforms one quiet Sunday morning when the shed was absolutely 'packed out' with locomotives. I still have a record of locomotives 'on shed' on 3rd June 1961 and the list includes representatives of many steam classes ranging from larger machines such as B1 4-6-0s and WD 2-8-0s to small tank classes, examples being J50 and J69 0-6-0Ts. A number of examples of Class N7 0-6-2Ts and L1 2-6-4Ts were recorded which was not surprising because both classes were still employed on suburban work at that time. Rather menacingly, a large proportion of the locomotives on view were diesel types of various shapes and sizes and just over a year later steam traction was almost totally eclipsed on the Great Eastern lines in the London area and East Anglia.

A visit to Willesden shed produced a rewarding sight in the shape of BR Standard 'Britannia' Pacific No.70042 Lord Roberts and Stanier 'Jubilees' Nos.45603 Solomon Islands and 45669 Fisher but the most interesting engine on shed was undoubtedly 'Jubilee' No.45552 Silver Jubilee. Nearby Neasden depot, which supplied motive power for the former Great Central route to Sheffield, still retained a LNER atmosphere with three of Gresley's Class V2 2-6-2s on shed together with a B1 4-6-0 and a K3 2-6-0.

During the compilation of this book I have received considerable assistance from Richard Barber (Armstrong Railway Photographic Trust), John Chalcraft (Rail Photoprints), Paul Chancellor (Colour Rail.com), Rodney Lissenden (R.C.Riley/Ken Wightman collection) and Peter Waller (Online Transport Archive). In addition Bob Dalton, Chris Evans, Dave Fakes and Terry Phillips have scrutinised the proof and made many constructive criticisms and comments that have undoubtedly improved the end product, and thanks are due to those gentlemen. I would also like to express my appreciation to the individual photographers who have kindly trusted me with their precious original colour transparencies, many of which are now more than 50 years old.

Michael Welch
Burgess Hill
West Sussex
June 2020

Paddington - an outstanding terminal station. The Great Western Railway's (GWR) ambitious plan to construct a railway from London to Bristol received the Royal Assent on 31st August 1835 and included a terminus at Euston which it proposed to share with the London & Birmingham Railway (L&BR). The L&BR used the standard gauge track, however, and were unhappy about sharing the station with the broad gauge GWR which decided to buy land at Paddington where a temporary terminus at Bishops Bridge Road was brought into use on 4th August 1838. On 13th June 1842 Queen Victoria made her first train journey from Slough to London after a trip to Windsor Castle and alighted at Bishops Bridge Road. The temporary terminus was clearly inadequate and Isambard Kingdom Brunel, engineer to the GWR, was no doubt pleased when the directors authorised expenditure on a new terminus at Paddington. The new station was designed by Brunel and the roof consisted of three arches, the widest spanning 102 ft 6 in and 54 ft high. There were offices alongside Platform 1, the traffic department occupying the ground floor while the upper floors were set aside for GWR management. Brunel's stroke of genius was his decision to contract Matthew Digby-Wyatt, who had been involved in the design work for the Crystal Palace, to embellish the new station with fine ornamentation. An innovation was the construction of two transepts running across the station and ending with decorative oriel windows from where the directors could observe the platforms. The new premises opened in 1854 together with the adjacent Great Western Royal hotel while in 1880 electric lighting was introduced at the terminus. Work on an extension to the premises, involving the building of another roof span, started in 1915 but had to be suspended for the duration of the war, but this addition lacked some of the intricate decoration of the earlier work. Between 1932 and 1934 the station and its approaches were resignalled with power operated colour light signals and many platforms extended to cope with longer trains, giving a remarkable total platform length of almost three miles. Here, an unidentified 6100 Class 2-6-2T poses amid the magnificent surroundings of Paddington station in the mid-1960s. *Robert Mitchell*

A group of train spotters, including one on a bicycle, congregate around 6100 Class 2-6-2T No.6156 at the end of one of Paddington station's long platforms on 30th July 1964. The locomotive's fireman is placing a headlamp on the coal bunker's top bracket before taking the empty stock of a main line arrival to the carriage sidings. The carriage visible in the photograph is a BR Standard Brake Composite Corridor (BCK) which is carrying waist-height destination boards, a feature peculiar to the Western Region (WR). When this scene was recorded the end of steam traction at Paddington was imminent and the traditionally impeccable standard of locomotive cleanliness had slipped considerably, to which the filthy condition of No.6156 bears ample testament. *Rail Photoprints*

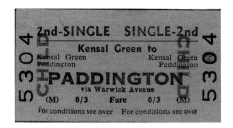

The complicated layout at the approach to Paddington is depicted in this view of 9400 Class 0-6-0PT No.9405 bringing a train of empty coaches into the station to form a main line departure; this picture was taken in September 1964. The large building on the right housed a goods depot while the girder bridge carries Westbourne Terrace across the tracks. No.9405 was one of a class that totalled 210 locomotives introduced by Hawksworth in 1947 so it was quite a modern design. Most of the locomotives comprising this class were built by outside contractors but No.9405 was a 'genuine article', having been out-shopped from Swindon works in May 1947. Some of the later batches were built by the Yorkshire Engine Company in 1956 and were the last machines of pre-nationalisation design to be constructed, one of which achieved only six years of service before being withdrawn. *Roy Denison*

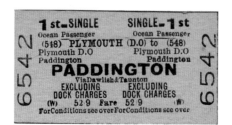

Gleaming BR Standard Pacific No.70016 *Ariel* from Cardiff (Canton) shed gets into its stride past Ladbroke Grove with the 1.55pm Paddington to Pembroke Dock train on 19th October 1957. This train also conveyed a portion to Neyland and was advertised to include a restaurant car as far as Swansea (High Street). Note that the formation is made up of a rake of BR Standard coaches in carmine and cream livery rather than 'chocolate and cream'. Later in its career No.70016 was transferred to the London Midland Region (LMR) and saw stints at Llandudno Junction and Aston (Birmingham) depots before being moved to Carlisle (Kingmoor) shed from where it was withdrawn in August 1967. *R.C.Riley*

One of the principal problems concerning the operation of Paddington station in former years was the need for light engines and empty trains to and from Old Oak Common to cross the running lines and in 1909 work commenced to improve the layout. This involved rebuilding no fewer that ten bridges between the terminus and Old Oak Common with a view to widening the approaches, remodelling of Westbourne Park station and construction of a new flyover near Old Oak Common to provide easier access to the depot and reduce conflicting movements. Unfortunately, the First World War intervened and the operation was not completed until 1928, and by that time no fewer than 350 sets of points had been installed, seven miles of plain track laid and a further eight miles of track had either been slewed or lifted. In this photograph 'Castle' Class 4-6-0 No.7004 *Eastnor Castle* is seen gathering speed after departure from Paddington with the 11.15am to Worcester on 27th August 1962. The flyover is visible in the background of this picture but the Grand Union Canal is out of sight behind the wall on the left, while a locomotive of London Midland & Scottish Railway (LMS) design stands at the head of an empty coal train. The school holidays would have been in full swing at this time of year and a number of young men in the foreground, some of whom are sitting dangerously close to the running lines, admire the 'Castle' class engine as it passes. *Martin Smith*

Introduced in 1919 during the Churchward era, the 4700 Class was designed as a mixed traffic type but primarily intended for heavy goods work. No.4700 was the first to appear in March 1919 and initially had a small boiler but this was replaced by a larger size boiler in 1921; Nos.4701 to 4708 were built with the large size boiler in 1922/23. These locomotives weighed 82 tons, had 5 ft 8 ins diameter driving wheels and possessed a tractive effort of 30,460 lb. No.4700 was exhibited at the Railway Centenary at Darlington in 1925. *Rail Photoprints*

During the dying days of BR steam traction the focus was firmly on the introduction of diesel motive power and maintenance of steam motive power depots was a long way down BR's list of priorities. Many sheds were woefully neglected with soot encrusted walls and dilapidated roofs that sometimes seemed so fragile they appeared to be in imminent danger of collapse. This picture shows the interior of Old Oak Common shed on 5th September 1964 and even at this late stage of the run-down of steam traction it is clear that at least some effort was, commendably, being made to keep the premises looking relatively clean and tidy and it was, perhaps, one of the better sheds in that respect. The locomotives seen here represented two generations of GWR-designed pannier tank engines: No.9707, on the left of the shot, was one of eleven locomotives built in the early 1930s and fitted with condensing apparatus for working over the Metropolitan Line to Smithfield. While it is not immediately apparent from the photograph it was equipped with a Weir feed pump (partially visible on the left) and also pannier tanks that were extended at the rear down to the running plate. No.9498 in contrast was one of the very last machines built to a pre-nationalisation design to enter traffic on BR, being built by the Yorkshire Engine Company in March 1955. Sadly, it lasted less than ten years in service, being withdrawn in September 1964. *R.C.Riley*

An unidentified westbound passenger train, comprised of a motley rake of stock, passes West Ealing behind BR Standard 'Britannia' Class 7P/6F Pacific No.70027 *Rising Star* on 1st June 1957. The tracks to Greenford can be seen diverging on the left of the shot while visible in the background are the signal box, and the station buildings located on a bridge. The busy coal yard can be seen on the right. *Rising Star* was one of 15 'Britannias' based at Cardiff (Canton) shed at that time primarily for use on Paddington expresses. *R.C.Riley*

Looking grimy and unkempt, 'Modified Hall' 4-6-0 No.7922 *Salford Hall* is depicted at West Ealing in charge of an up goods working on 7th September 1964. The writing was very much on the wall for WR steam traction by that date and the glory days of gleaming copper-capped chimneys were becoming a distant memory as the pace of withdrawals was unrelenting. Built at Swindon in September 1950, No.7922 was destined to soldier on until the very last days of WR steam traction in December 1965. *Martin Smith*

An unidentified 'Britannia' Pacific passes Hanwell with the London-bound 'Capitals United Express' on a sunny morning some time in the late 1950s/early 1960s. The uniform 'chocolate and cream' set of coaches has been marred by the inclusion of a few vehicles in carmine and cream or maroon livery. In the 1961 summer timetable the up working started at Swansea (High Street), from where it departed at 6.30am, and was scheduled to arrive in London at 10.55am. The down train departed from Paddington at 3.55pm calling at Cardiff (General) at 6.53pm before continuing to Fishguard Harbour; this train also conveyed through carriages to Haverfordwest and Neyland. *Ken Wightman*

Seventy of these workmanlike 6100 Class 2-6-2Ts were introduced in 1931 primarily for working suburban services in the London area and in this illustration No.6108 is seen at Hanwell in 1959. The locomotives were designed by Collett, weighed 78 tons 9 cwt, and possessed a tractive effort of 27,340lb. They were largely displaced by diesel units in the late 1950s but continued to be a regular sight in the London area on miscellaneous passenger and empty stock duties almost until the end of WR steam traction in late 1965. A small number of these engines found their way into south Wales and the Gloucester area but they will always be remembered for their work in the capital. Out-shopped from Swindon in May 1931, No.6108 remained in traffic until it was withdrawn in August 1965. *Barry Blacklock*

An intruder on the former GWR main line. On 24th June 1962 the Home Counties Railway Club organised a special train from Paddington to Swindon for a visit to the works and the newly opened GWR museum. The motive power requested was 'Lord Nelson' Class 7P 4-6-0 No.30850 *Lord Nelson* which is seen here crossing Hanwell viaduct; note the coat of arms on the left hand side of the viaduct. The locomotive arrived at Paddington the wrong way round and had to make the short trip to Ranelagh Bridge for turning, and as a result the train departed 16 minutes late. Most of the 16 members of this class had already been withdrawn by the date of the photograph and No.30850 was withdrawn for preservation only two months after this picture was taken; the last survivors were taken out of traffic in October 1962. When they were built the 'Lord Nelson's were the most powerful locomotives in Great Britain but quickly lost their crown to the GWR's 'King' Class 4-6-0s. *Martin Smith*

Photographed from an ideally situated footbridge which provided a panoramic view of train movements, the 6.38pm from Paddington to High Wycombe, formed of five non-corridor vehicles, is seen approaching Southall station with Collett 6100 Class 2-6-2T No.6169 in charge in the evening sunshine on 27th June 1961. This train was one of a small number of mainly rush-hour services that provided a through London service to the branch stations between Bourne End and High Wycombe, the advertised arrival time at the latter place being 7.58pm. Southall motive power depot is visible in the centre of the picture with the branch to Brentford curving away to the right. Services along the Brentford line were withdrawn temporarily during the First World War and the branch lost its trains for a second time in May 1942 but on that occasion they were not reinstated, but the line remained open for goods traffic. Diesel units were in use on many suburban routes from Paddington by the date of this photograph and two can just be discerned in the background.
Martin Smith

A further shot of a 6100 Class 2-6-2T at Southall, this time taken in June 1960, showing the strategic footbridge from where the previous picture was taken; the locomotive is No.6152 but the identity of the train is not known. Two items of the paraphernalia of the steam age, the water crane and its attendant 'fire devil', are visible at the platform end. The signalling at Southall at this time appears to have been a combination of two-aspect colour light and semaphore, the signal box being partially visible on the right of the photograph. Some of the branches in the London area were worked by former Great Western railcars and two of those vehicles can just be seen in the background. Most of the railcars were based in the Worcester area but half a dozen operated in the London area.
Barry Blacklock

The bulk of main line services from Paddington to Bristol, south Wales and the West Country ran via Reading, but there was also an hourly service on the route to Birmingham (Snow Hill) and Wolverhampton (Low Level). Some trains on this line travelled way beyond the West Midlands and provided valuable through services to the Welsh coast and Birkenhead (Woodside) via Shrewsbury. Regrettably, this through route was destroyed in the over zealous rationalisation of the late 1960s when this traffic was concentrated on London (Euston), the Snow Hill to Wolverhampton section now being part of the West Midlands tram network. This route hosted some prestigious named trains such as the 'Cambrian Coast Express' and diesel-worked 'Birmingham Pullman' but the 4.15pm Paddington to Banbury, which was formed of only five coaches when this shot was taken on 4th October 1963 at Park Royal, was clearly not among them. The locomotive in view is 'Hall' Class 4-6-0 No.4988 *Bulwell Hall* which is in extremely grimy condition. The track in the foreground is an industrial branch while London Transport's Central Line tracks to West Ruislip are visible with the route to Ealing Broadway curving away sharply on the extreme right. The scrap metal dealers Cox and Danks, whose site dominates the area behind the train, were not averse to breaking-up withdrawn BR steam locomotives and one wonders whether *Bulwell Hall* was among them. *Martin Smith*

Railway enthusiasts always dream of an impressive smoke effect when they are taking a picture but here the fortunate photographer has clearly arrived just at the right time to record a trackside blaze which is producing more smoke than 'King' Class 4-6-0 No.6021 *King Richard II* passing at the head of the 12.10pm Paddington to Birkenhead (Woodside). What brilliant timing! This scene was recorded at Hanger Lane on 20th July 1962. The 'Kings' were introduced in 1927 and when they were built they were the most powerful locomotives in Great Britain, enabling the proud GWR to snatch back the honour of owning the most powerful engines from the Southern Railway, whose 'Lord Nelson' class had only recently been introduced. When this picture was taken, however, the 'Kings' were facing imminent extinction due to the mass invasion of 'Western' class diesel hydraulic locomotives on which crew training was in full swing. Some members of the class had already been withdrawn and when the diesels took over the bulk of the locomotive diagrams on this route from 10th September 1962 no fewer than 13 'Kings', including No.6021, were immediately taken out of service and all had gone by the end of the year. The 'Kings' had all been deposed - a very sad outcome for devotees of Great Western steam. *Martin Smith*

Marylebone – the Cinderella of all the London terminal stations. In the mid-nineteenth century the Manchester, Sheffield & Lincolnshire Railway (MSLR) was one of the smaller companies operating across the north of England and for a time Sir Edward Watkin was its energetic chairman. He was determined to expand the railway's system and in March 1893 the MSLR obtained an Act of Parliament authorising a new line from Annesley, near Nottingham, to Quainton Road, Buckinghamshire, where a connection with the Metropolitan Railway was proposed. The new route, which was known as the 'London Extension', opened in March 1899 to a modest terminus at Marylebone, by which time the MSLR had changed its name to the much grander title of 'Great Central Railway' (GCR). The status of the MSLR had been transformed overnight from a provincial cross-country line to a major trunk route but, alas, the GCR never achieved the success envisaged by its promoters. Most of the intermediate places it served already had services to London and, even worse, the GCR traversed a 45 miles-long stretch of middle England between Rugby and Aylesbury that was very thinly populated and offered little traffic potential. The Marylebone terminus was compact and very quiet compared to other London stations but boasted a sumptuous railway hotel and a delightful porte-cochere which was an architectural gem. The hotel later became railway offices and was latterly the headquarters of the British Railways Board, known unromantically as '222 Marylebone Road'. In the 1950s BR was in a precarious financial position and sought to eliminate so-called 'duplicate routes', and the GC line was earmarked for closure along much of its length. This process began in earnest in 1958 when the LMR took over administration of the line from the ER and it lost no time in discouraging traffic. The through trains to Manchester via Sheffield (Victoria) ceased in early 1960 and March 1963 saw the withdrawal of local trains between Aylesbury and Sheffield, and the last daytime Sunday service north of Aylesbury. In June 1965 the writing was really on the wall when through freight traffic was diverted to other routes and the inevitable closure north of Aylesbury occurred in September 1966 except for a work people's service grudgingly provided between Rugby and Nottingham. Towards the end the principal long distance service consisted of three weekday trains between Marylebone and Nottingham, usually worked by steam locomotives with at least one wheel in the scrapyard. Here a Nottingham Victoria train is seen awaiting departure from Marylebone with Stanier Class 5MT No.44847 in charge on 16th August 1966, just a few weeks before the service was withdrawn. *David Wigley*

Marylebone station's relative quietness and appealing Victorian atmosphere ensured its popularity with film makers and in this fascinating picture BR Standard Class 3MT No.82019 is seen simmering during a filming session on 25th June 1967. A sequence was being filmed for 'Star – The Gertrude Lawrence Story' starring Julie Andrews, Bruce Forsyth, Beryl Reid and Jenny Agutter. The locomotive is standing at the head of a really vintage rake of coaches which had apparently been hired by the film company from the Longmoor Military Railway in Hampshire. The inclusion of a freight brake van at both ends of the train indicates that the coaches may not have been fitted with vacuum brakes. Regular steam traction had become a thing of the past at Marylebone following the closure of most of the GC line so No.82019 was brought across from Nine Elms to fill the breach. Like so many locomotives in BR service it had lost its front number plate by this date and, indeed, the elimination of steam at Nine Elms and in the entire London area occurred just three weeks after this shot was taken. At least No.82019 had benefited from being spruced up for its starring role. *David Wigley*

The station canopy at Marylebone neatly frames Stanier Class 5MT No.45299 as it comes to rest with the 8.15am train from Nottingham on 26th July 1965. By the date of this photograph three daytime semi-fast Marylebone-Nottingham trains (and vice versa) comprised the principal services along the GC route, as previously mentioned, and some of those consisted of only four coaches, as seen here. The 8.15am was booked to cover the 126½ miles between the two cities in 3 hours 10 minutes and stopped at all the major intermediate stations that remained open, including the smaller stations of East Leake, Ashby Magna and Lutterworth. *Rail Photoprints*

Next stop Harrow-on-the-Hill! Stanier Class 5MT 4-6-0 No.44847 is depicted leaving Marylebone with the train seen in a previous picture. While passenger services from there along the GC line were a pale shadow of former years, in the mid-1960s Marylebone station played host to a number of services diverted from the West Coast Main Line (WCML) which was in the throes of electrification work. The winter 1964-65 timetable advertised the 12.15am to Manchester Piccadilly where it was due to arrive at 5.01am. This service also called intermediately at Crewe so presumably took the spur at Calvert to gain access to the WCML at Bletchley. Another overnight service was the 9.55pm (10.45pm on Saturdays) to Manchester Piccadilly which at least took the traditional route via Sheffield Victoria and called only at the major intermediate stations on the route; this was presumably mainly a newspaper/parcels train with only limited seating accommodation. Ironically, in its heyday some of Marylebone's principal services were those to Manchester but by 1965 only a rump survived as a reminder of times past. *David Wigley*

BR Standard Class 3MT No.82019 leaves Marylebone hauling a most remarkable ensemble of vintage rolling stock on 25th June 1967. The first and third carriages are former South Eastern & Chatham Railway 'Birdcage' brake vehicles while the coach marshalled between them appears to be an inspection saloon. Two members of this class of 2-6-2Ts survived on the 'Southern' until the end of steam and it is recorded that No.82019 was employed as a station pilot at Waterloo on Saturday 8th July 1967, the penultimate day of steam on the SR, while sister locomotive No.82029, most unusually, was put to work on the 7.18am Waterloo to Salisbury passenger service. After this unaccustomed main line duty No.82029 retired to the dump at Salisbury shed where the remaining steam motive power was being congregated prior to disposal and was, no doubt, later joined by No.82019. *David Wigley*

The tracks of London Transport's Neasden station dominate the background as the 4.38pm Marylebone to Nottingham Victoria train passes behind Stanier Class 5MT No.45088 on 30th July 1963. Some train formations on the GC main line had been reduced to a mere four coaches by this date but the 4.38pm was virtually a 'rush hour' service and warranted six. The bracket signal's indication is 'off' for a train along the main line while the signals at danger refer to the route towards Northolt Junction where connection was made with the GWR Paddington to Birmingham Snow Hill line. The tracks veering off to the right in the picture connected with the goods only route from Cricklewood to Acton Wells Junction, where the North London line was joined. *Martin Smith*

A Nottingham Victoria to Marylebone train passes Harrow-on-the-Hill on 30th December 1963 behind 'Royal Scot' Class 4-6-0 No.46125 *3rd Carabinier*. Annesley shed, north of Nottingham, which provided motive power for the residual GC line passenger service, had an allocation of those locomotives. In late 1962 a batch of four 'Royal Scots' was transferred to Annesley and by the end of the year their allocation had grown to nine machines. It was sometimes alleged that locomotives in a bad state that were working out their mileage prior to withdrawal were earmarked for Annesley. The provision of passenger locomotives in reasonable condition was apparently not high on the LMR's priority list in view of their wish to withdraw the service. Certainly, No.46125 appears to be in a terrible state in this photograph so perhaps the rumours that the GC was allocated engines in the worst mechanical condition were not just idle gossip. *Martin Smith*

Most railway photographers in the London area were drawn to the main line tracks where the more glamorous long distance expresses could be seen and the mundane goods workings in the capital were frequently overlooked. In this portrait Urie Class S15 No.30503 is depicted on a cross-London freight train between Willesden Junction and Acton Central stations on 23rd April 1963. This locomotive was one of the very sizeable number of Class S15 locomotives allocated to Feltham shed and the huge marshalling yard at that location was the train's most likely destination. The last five surviving Class S15s were taken out of traffic in September 1965 but No.30837 was retained for a Locomotive Club of Great Britain rail tour which was so heavily patronised it ran on two successive Sundays in January 1966. *Martin Smith*

Euston station boasted one of the most splendid monuments of the railway age while at the same time was notorious as one of the dowdiest and appallingly laid out main line terminal stations. The 112 miles-long London and Birmingham Railway (L&BR), engineered by Robert Stephenson, was one of the early trunk lines that captured the imagination of the general public. Approved by Parliament in 1833 the route was opened from Euston to Boxmoor on 20th July 1837 with the full service throughout to Birmingham commencing on 17th September 1838. The L&BR decided to create a landmark that would provide an impressive entrance to the station and Philip Hardwick designed a huge Greek-style Doric Arch, or portico, which stood away from the train shed across a courtyard and appeared rather incongruous to some observers. While the entrance to the station may have been a magnificent symbol of the new, exciting railway era Euston station, which had only two platforms at that time, was a definite anti-climax. When the station opened trains were hauled by ropes attached to a stationary winding engine located at the top of Camden bank and it was 1844 before the first locomotives penetrated to Euston. Additional traffic arising from connections with the Midland Counties Railway at Rugby prompted the addition in 1840 of two new platforms to cater for this traffic and as it was possible to reach the north-east of England by this route they were known as the 'York' platforms, a nickname that survived well into BR days. Construction of the range of buildings behind the portico began in 1846 including the Great Hall, one of the architectural gems of the railway age, and thereafter Euston station grew on a chaotic, piecemeal basis. In 1870-73 more arrival platforms were provided while there was further expansion in the early-1890s. Some platforms were extended to cope with longer train formations, notably in 1935 and 1952. In the twilight years of the old station there were 15 platforms, Nos. 1 to 3 being for main line arrivals while Nos. 12 to 15 were the principal main line departure platforms. In between there was a jumble of shorter platforms generally used for local and medium distance services while Nos.10 and 11 were designated for parcels traffic only. The London Midland & Scottish Railway formulated plans to rebuild the station in the late-1930s but the Second World War intervened and reconstruction at last went ahead in the early 1960s as part of the modernisation of the West Coast Main Line. The authorities stated that it would not be possible to construct a station large enough for modern needs without demolishing the celebrated Doric Arch and Great Hall and this controversial proposal provoked an outcry. Despite pleas from historians and academics the decision to knock down two of the most magnificent buildings of the Victorian age was upheld by Harold Macmillan, the Prime Minister at the time, and demolition of the arch commenced immediately and had been completed by the end of 1961. While the new station that emerged is undoubtedly much easier to operate today the main building, opened by Queen Elizabeth II on 14th October 1968, is soulless and already looking tired and dated. Here Stanier Class 5MT No. 45331 sits at the buffer stops at Euston after arrival from the north in the early 1960s, the dark and somewhat dingy atmosphere of the place being all too apparent. *Tim Stephens*

A crane, in the background of this scene, hovers above the skeleton of the 'new' Euston as it arises from the rubble of the old station; this picture was taken on 30th July 1964. The principal subject in this shot is Stanier Class 6P/5F 'Jubilee' 4-6-0 No.45604 *Ceylon* which is in dreadful external condition and is presumably waiting to take a train northwards. While the station was being rebuilt many services were diverted to other routes, and frequencies increased where possible, with Paddington becoming the principal London terminal station for passengers heading for the west Midlands while the service from St Pancras to Manchester was also augmented. It was not practicable to divert London to Holyhead trains, such as the 'Emerald Isle Express' seen at the adjacent platform, and these continued to serve Euston. *Rail Photoprints*

Euston station, going, going, almost gone. The 2.00pm to Liverpool Lime Street, with 'Royal Scot' Class 7P 4-6-0 No.46168 *The Girl Guide* in charge, awaits departure from Euston on 26th May 1963. Reconstruction of the station started in 1963 and by the time this photograph was taken much of the arrivals side had already been reduced to rubble and new steelwork erected. The departures side of the station appears to be more or less intact in this shot but it is recorded that demolition of the Great Hall, one of the architectural masterpieces of the railway age, took place two months after this picture was taken. On the right of the picture an English Electric Type 4 diesel locomotive waits at an adjacent platform with another train to the north. *Rail Photoprints*

Euston station's higgledy-piggledy roof line provides an immediate clue to its haphazard development over many years – the authorities simply added new buildings to the existing premises as adjacent land became available. One of the major drawbacks was the location of the Great Hall which divided the station into two parts, a situation that was never overcome until the rebuilding of the 1960s. In this illustration, which was taken in the early 1960s during the transition from steam to diesel traction, the variety of motive power that operated from Euston can be seen. Electric multiple units on Watford services are visible in Platform Nos. 4 and 5 and Fairburn Class 4MT 2-6-4T No.42099 is captured making a brisk getaway from Platform 6 with an outer suburban train while a BR/Sulzer Type 2 diesel locomotive sits in Platform 9 with another passenger working. Platform 10 was set aside for parcels traffic and piles of parcels plus a BR road van are just visible. The tall section of roof on the right covered the departure platforms which were completed in 1892 after the railway company obtained an Act of Parliament to permit the diversion of Cardington Street and acquisition of the burial ground of St James's church. The latter had to be excavated and coffins removed to Finchley cemetery. *RCTS Archive*

The severity of the climb away from Euston can also be appreciated in this shot of Fairburn Class 4MT 2-6-4T No.42066 passing Camden No.1 signal box with a train of empty stock on 21st June 1962. A real effort had apparently been made to smarten up the locomotive's side tanks and bunker but the rest of the locomotive is rather dirty. *Rail Photoprints*

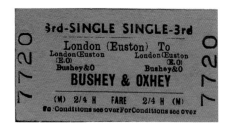

Opposite: Originally the L&BR planned a terminus at Camden, which at that time was on the edge of open country, and it was decided that one closer to London was desirable. Throughout most of its existence Euston has been in a constant state of upheaval and extensions and, ironically, the station's site was itself at the end of the extension from Camden. Constructing the last mile or so of the route into Euston was not without its difficulties, however, because Camden was on much higher ground and the Act of Parliament authorising the extension contained clauses to prevent interference with traffic on the nearby Regent's canal. The local topography, coupled with the requirement to clear the canal, necessitated a gradient of 1 in 77 which presented a challenge to generations of enginemen starting from Euston with a 'cold' engine and trains were often assisted at the rear. Here 'The Merseyside Express', headed by Stanier 'Princess Royal' Pacific No.46203 *Princess Margaret Rose*, ascends the bank on the first stage of the journey to Liverpool in 1957. There were three titled express trains linking London with Liverpool Lime Street in the late 1950s and in the 1959/60 timetable this particular train was scheduled to leave London at 6.00pm and it arrived in Liverpool at 10.15pm. Through carriages were conveyed to Southport Chapel Street where the advertised arrival time was 10.54pm. *Rail Photoprints*

A Stanier Pacific – pride of the West Coast Main Line. Railway historians have their allegiances but most agree that Sir William Stanier's celebrated 'Princess Coronation' Pacifics were among the finest, if not the finest, express passenger steam locomotives built in Great Britain. Here, beautifully prepared No.46248 *City of Leeds* makes a memorable sight at the top of Camden bank on 6th June 1962. The roof of Camden No.1 signal box can just be seen above the second coach of this express, believed to be 'The Northern Irishman', the 7.25pm Euston to Stranraer Harbour, and in steam days it must have been a welcome sight for crews of locomotives struggling up the bank, but No.46248 appears to be making an effortless climb. Note the formation of the train which includes a restaurant car immediately behind the locomotive; this was hardly the best position for such a vehicle and its occupants would have suffered a particularly bumpy ride in addition to smoke occasionally pouring through the open windows. The restaurant car was probably detached when engines were changed at Crewe, so was marshalled immediately behind the locomotive for operating convenience. Passengers sitting towards the middle of the train would have had to negotiate their way through at least two guards' brake vans, one of which is adjacent to the restaurant car. Perhaps a minor inconvenience when one considers they were being hauled by *City of Leeds*. *Rail Photoprints*

Another shot taken close to Camden No.1 signal box, with Camden goods depot dominating the background. In this illustration BR Standard 'Britannia' Pacific No.70021 *Morning Star*, in quite clean external condition, is depicted at the head of an unidentified down train on 21st July 1962. *Morning Star* was a former Western Region locomotive allocated to Plymouth Laira in the early 1950s, followed by Cardiff Canton. It later moved to the LMR and was on the books at Trafford Park (Manchester) shed for a while before moving to Willesden where it was based at the time of this photograph. No.70021's career ended at Carlisle Kingmoor shed at the end of December 1967 when it was among the last surviving batch of 'Britannias'. *Rail Photoprints*

The 12.45pm Euston to Blackpool train, powered by 'Royal Scot' 4-6-0 No.46129 *The Scottish Horse*, speeds away from Kensal Green tunnel on 3rd June 1963. This location would probably have looked very different if the GWR's proposal to converge with the LBR at Kensal Green and share Euston station had come to fruition, but the former's choice of the seven foot gauge put paid to this fanciful idea and probably just as well – how on earth would Euston have coped? There was originally a single tunnel here but a third track through a separate tunnel was opened in July 1858 and in 1875 a fourth track was laid but gauntleted through the 1858 tunnel until a new bore came into use in June 1879. The London & North Western Railway (LNWR) was slow to develop suburban traffic, but by 1900 this was increasing and the company started work on the 'New Lines' (two additional running lines) to develop this traffic to Willesden and beyond. It was agreed that Bakerloo Line underground trains would share those tracks and on 11th February 1915 the latter was extended to Queen's Park, but the full service to Euston was deferred until 1922 by which time a new tunnel and extensive track alterations had been completed around Primrose Hill. *Martin Smith*

The maintenance of steam locomotives was always a laborious and dirty task and motive power depots, as the engine sheds were officially known, could also be dangerous places to work as exemplified here by the slippery surface and open inspection pits in this picture taken at Willesden shed on 15th July 1964. The subject of this portrait is BR Standard 'Britannia' Pacific No.70021 *Morning Star*, a resident of Willesden depot which had a total of nine 'Britannias' on its books at this time. The locomotive, fitted with a 1A shed allocation plate, bears evidence of recent cleaning and still has its nameplates in place so it looks reasonably presentable. The locomotive lurking just inside the shed is a 'Princess Coronation' class in its last few months of service. Willesden was host to express passenger classes following the closure of Camden in 1963 but throughout its life was noted as the home of dozens of freight engines and in 1948 no fewer than 35 Stanier Class 8Fs were allocated plus 18 former LNWR 7Fs. A small number of 'Patriots' and 'Jubilees' were also based there at that time but these totalled only 7 engines. *David Wigley*

When asked to compile a list of the locomotives with the most character and distinguishing features the average railway enthusiast would nominate the streamlined Class A4s or air-smoothed Bulleid Pacifics, and the LNWR 'Super Ds' would probably be overlooked. After all, they were the unglamorous workhorses of heavy freight haulage and never set any speed records, but they were one of the very few classes of 0-8-0 tender locomotives with inside cylinders, had very unusual spoked driving wheels and, strangely, were never fitted with BR smokebox numberplates. This photograph of No.49377 hauling a massive 74-wagon goods train was taken at Wembley on 13th April 1962 and vividly illustrates the considerable haulage capacity of these machines, their tractive effort being only marginally below that of the Stanier Class 8F 2-8-0s which belong to a much later generation of steam traction. No.49377 was built in 1902 and underwent various modifications during its long career which ended in October 1962. A true, very distinctive veteran of a class that never rose to fame. *Martin Smith*

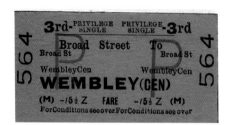

Hauling a massive load of 14 carriages comprising the 6.10pm Euston to Liverpool 'The Merseyside Express', Stanier 'Princess Royal' Pacific No.46208 *Princess Helena Victoria* is getting into its stride near Wembley in May 1962. In early 1961 the entire 'Princess Royal' class had been put into store as 'surplus to requirements' but most re-entered traffic for the summer service, after which six were withdrawn while the remainder returned to store. There was a motive power crisis in early 1962 and the six remaining locomotives were again returned to service. Their reprieve lasted until the autumn of that year when all of the survivors were taken out of service. No.46209 *Princess Beatrice* was the first to go, in September 1962, while four of its sister locomotives were withdrawn during the following month. No.46200 *The Princess Royal* managed to evade the withdrawal orders and continued at work from Carlisle Kingmoor shed for a few more weeks – a sad end to an outstanding class. *Martin Smith*

Authorised as a replacement for 'Princess Royal' Pacific No.46202 *Princess Anne*, which was damaged beyond repair in the Harrow crash on 8th October 1952, BR Standard Pacific No.71000 *Duke of Gloucester* was disappointing in service. No.71000, intended to be the prototype for a new design for express passenger duties, was a three cylinder locomotive with Caprotti valve gear which was nominally more powerful than the 'Britannia' Pacifics and was the most powerful BR Standard passenger locomotive. *Duke of Gloucester* was built at Crewe and entered traffic in 1954, the year before the modernisation plan was unveiled which heralded the eventual withdrawal of steam traction. Inevitably, it remained the sole representative of its class, and the idea of constructing a series of locomotives based on the same design was quietly abandoned in view of impending dieselisation. While it became something of a 'white elephant' it did at least achieve the somewhat dubious distinction of being the very last express passenger locomotive to be built in Great Britain. Withdrawn in November 1962 after a very short operational career, No.71000's cylinders and motion were salvaged for preservation while the remains were despatched to Barry scrapyard. *Duke of Gloucester* was later saved for preservation and during the course of its protracted and painstaking restoration it was discovered that mistakes had been made during its construction and areas of the original specification overlooked which may have accounted for its lacklustre performance in everyday service. No.71000 is seen here at North Wembley on 31st May 1962 hauling the northbound 'Northern Irishman' which linked Euston and Stranraer Harbour and was, in effect, a boat train for sailings to Northern Ireland. *Martin Smith*

During the height of summer the light is at its best in the early morning or before dusk, if the sun is shining of course, and this attractive image provides ample proof of that assertion. Here, 'Royal Scot' Class 7P 4-6-0 No.46128 *The Lovat Scouts* is seen speeding towards London near South Kenton in beautiful early morning sunshine at 7.15am on 17th July 1962. The train is an overnight express from Perth to London and the passenger vehicles formed immediately behind the locomotive are sleeping cars – how on earth could people get any sleep with a 'Royal Scot' blasting away at the front of the train! Surely, the photographer deserves a special commendation for getting up so early to take this memorable shot and, perhaps, those passengers who managed to get some sleep. *Martin Smith*

Stanier's Pacifics – the pride of the West Coast Main Line. Another early morning picture, this time taken near Kenton station, showing 'Princess Coronation' Pacific No.46238 *City of Carlisle* heading towards London on the last stage of the journey from Stranraer Harbour to the capital with the up 'Northern Irishman'. This shot was taken in soft morning sunshine at 8.08am on 7th July 1962. In the background an electric unit, probably forming a train from Watford, can just be discerned. *Martin Smith*

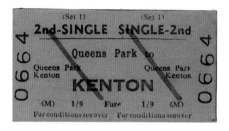

An up express, with 'Princess Royal' Class Pacific No.46204 *Princess Louise* in charge, speeds along the fast line between Hatch End and Headstone Lane on 20th February 1954. *Princess Louise* was built at Crewe, entered traffic in July 1935 and lasted until October 1961 when it became one of the first victims of the dieselisation of the WCML. The electrified tracks on the left carry Watford suburban trains and at the time of this photograph they were also used by Bakerloo Line services but these days Bakerloo trains no longer run beyond Harrow & Wealdstone. *Neil Davenport/Online Transport Archive*

An express bound for Euston speeds past Carpenders Park station some time in the late 1950s; motive power is provided by 'Royal Scot' Class 7P 4-6-0 No.46130 *The West Yorkshire Regiment*. This locomotive had an amazingly nomadic career and at various times was based at sheds in Leeds, Manchester, Liverpool plus London and was even on the books at Low Moor shed, near Bradford, for a brief period. No.46130 was withdrawn from Holbeck depot in Leeds in December 1962, a year that saw almost half of the locomotives of this celebrated class taken out of traffic. *Ken Wightman*

A brace of Stanier Class 5MT 4-6-0s heads north past Carpenders Park with a sleeping car leading: this photograph is thought to have been taken on 4th July 1959. Once again a sleeping car is marshalled immediately behind the locomotives – perhaps overnight travellers qualified for a refund if they didn't get any sleep. In the (totally unbiased!) author's opinion the 'Black Fives' were the answer to every enginemen's prayer and were economical, reliable and versatile, and probably cost a lot less to maintain than other, more complicated, steam locomotives. The Class 5MTs, which were constructed over a period of 16 years from 1935, worked in almost every corner of Great Britain from Stranraer to Margate and from Poole to Wick so nobody could possibly doubt their incredible versatility and, indeed, route availability. *Ken Wightman*

A line of trees provides an attractive setting for this shot of nicely cleaned Stanier 'Black Five' No.45111 as it heads north with a heavy freight in the evening sunshine at Carpenders Park; this picture is also thought to date from the late 1950s. *Ken Wightman*

Watford Junction station as you've probably never seen it before. A southbound train formed of LMS stock in carmine and cream livery and headed by the doyen of the 'Royal Scot' class, No.46100 *Royal Scot*, passes through the station on 19th March 1955. No.46100 bears a Camden (1B) shed plate so it didn't have far to go to its home depot. Note the motive power depot buildings behind the station nameboard on the right and smoke deflectors on the footbridge. Within a few years of this picture being taken this scene was transformed by the rebuilding of the station and electrification and makes one wonder: did it really used to look like that? *Royal Scot* was later saved for preservation by the late Sir Billy Butlin and has subsequently appeared on main line special workings. *Neil Davenport*

The Harrow & Wealdstone to Stanmore line is one of the few branch lines in the London area to have succumbed to closure. The branch was incorporated on the 25th June 1886 and opened on 18th December 1890, and its opening apparently prompted considerable growth of residential properties around the terminus. The line no doubt prospered until the Metropolitan Railway's extension from Wembley Park reached Stanmore on 10th December 1932, and this development marked the beginning of the end for the branch as the Metropolitan offered a direct and more frequent service to central London. The section north of the intermediate station of Belmont was closed from 15th September 1952 while the remaining stub lasted until 5th October 1964. In the early-1950s an experimental lightweight 3-car diesel unit underwent trials on the truncated branch and this was one of the few occasions when the branch was in the public eye. The compact little station at Stanmore was surrounded by trees which made photography tricky at the height of summer but the photographer has positioned himself perfectly to obtain this shot of No.40043 posing with the branch train some time during the summer of 1952. The young lad leaning from a window of the front coach is clearly fascinated by the antics of the photographer and one wonders how he would have reacted if told the picture was actually being taken in colour, that medium being very rare at the time. *Neil Davenport*

Prior to 1857 all the Midland Railway's (MR) traffic to London was worked along the line from Leicester to Rugby but during that year an extension southwards from Leicester was opened to Bedford and Hitchin, and from 1st February 1858 the MR began to work trains into King's Cross. The service was sparse, however, consisting of only seven departures a day by 1864 and independent access to the capital was clearly essential for the 'mighty' MR. On 22nd June 1863 a route was sanctioned from Bedford to a new passenger terminus on the Euston Road and the station was to be called St Pancras. Goods traffic to the adjacent yard began on 9th September 1867 and on 13th July 1868 a local passenger service commenced from Bedford to Moorgate which was then known as 'Moorgate Street'. The main St Pancras terminal station opened for business on 1st October 1868, and the MR had at last gained its own London station and no longer had to depend on the co-operation of rivals. The line had to gain height to cross the Regent's canal and continued at that level to Euston Road, the station being raised around 15 feet above street level with the space beneath the platforms being used for the storage of beer from Burton-on-Trent, that being an important source of revenue for the MR. The seven platforms were covered by a splendid 25,000 square foot glazed roof designed by W.H. Barlow with a single span of 240 feet. In 1903 there were 38 suburban and 28 main line departures from St Pancras but it should be borne in mind that many suburban workings by-passed the station and terminated at Moorgate. The former Midland Grand Hotel looms over the Euston Road, this being a three hundred-room Gothic Revival masterpiece designed by George Gilbert Scott who, despite his design being larger and more expensive than the brief, won a competition organised by the MR. His grandiose design incorporated new technology such as radiators and lifts, the latter being the first in London. The hotel closed in 1935, a victim of changing fashions, and became railway offices for a period before being abandoned and even threatened with demolition. It is today regarded by most architectural historians as one of Great Britain's most significant buildings and now enjoys a new lease of life as an exclusive hotel. Unlike the hotel's facade, steam trains were not widely photographed at St Pancras during the BR era but here is a shot of Stanier 'Jubilee' 4-6-0 No.45721 *Impregnable* waiting to leave the station with the Locomotive Club of Great Britain's 'North Countryman' rail tour on 6th June 1964. That locomotive hauled the train as far as Leeds where Gresley Class V2 2-6-2 No.60923 took over for a run over the Settle & Carlisle line. The V2 returned the train to Leeds via Shap, Low Gill and Settle Junction before giving way at Leeds to another Gresley-designed machine, Class A3 Pacific No.60051 *Blink Bonny* for trip down the East Coast Main Line to King's Cross. *RCTS Photo Archive*

A scene at the platform end of St Pancras station showing smartly turned out Stanier Class 5MT No.45221 apparently awaiting departure with a northbound express some time in the late 1950s. This machine was allocated to Leicester shed for a period in the 1950s so perhaps it was heading for that city. The locomotive looks really cared for which is more than can be said for the coach which is clearly overdue for attention with bare patches on the window mouldings where the paint has fallen off. The station was still mechanically signalled at the time of this photograph, an old wooden signal box and lower quadrant semaphores being visible. Today, St Pancras is an international transport hub, and Leicester is one of many destinations that can be reached from the station. *Ken Wightman*

The engine cleaners at Kentish Town shed have made a reasonable job of sprucing up Fairburn Class 4MT 2-6-4T No.42237 which was photographed waiting to haul a train of empty stock to the carriage sidings. This locomotive was out-shopped from Derby works in August 1946 and appears to have spent the greater part of its career based at Kentish Town shed but was withdrawn from Burton-on-Trent depot in December 1962. This picture was taken at St Pancras in the early 1960s. *Colour-Rail*

ST PANCRAS TO ELSTREE

Generations of station masters at St Pancras would, hopefully, have wanted the station to be kept in neat, tidy and clean condition but the never ending columns of black smoke being emitted by steam locomotives ensured that any hope of keeping the overall roof clean was a totally lost cause. Here the soot encrusted roof is clearly visible as Stanier 'Black Five' No.45274 awaits departure with a Nottingham train alongside 'Jubilee' No.45618 *New Hebrides* 'blowing off' at the head of an express to Manchester (Central). This photograph was taken in May 1958 when steam traction was very much 'king' at St. Pancras. *Colour-Rail*

The bright red headboard attached to the front of 'Jubilee' Class 4-6-0 No.45579 *Punjab* seems to emphasise the locomotive's disgraceful external condition – surely Kentish Town shed could have found a more presentable locomotive for such a high profile Anglo-Scottish train. This picture was taken in February 1960. *Colour-Rail*

A Bedford to St Pancras train, powered by Stanier Class 5MT 4-6-0 No.44822, is depicted at Cricklewood in 1959. Note that the formation is comprised almost entirely of non-corridor compartment stock. The winter 1959 timetable reveals an irregular stopping service from St Pancras to St Albans/Bedford with, strangely, a particularly long gap at the height of the rush-hour when two commuter trains ran from Moorgate to St Albans. There were, of course, express workings that called at St Albans, Harpenden and Luton only but the smaller intermediate stations were poorly served with 'all stations' trains taking as much as one hour and fifty-two minutes for the almost 50 miles-long St Pancras to Bedford journey. The local commuters were clearly disgruntled with such an unattractive timetable and in late 1956 held a meeting with Mr David Blee, General Manager, London Midland Region (LMR). Their complaints sparked the LMR's hierarchy into action and by the summer of 1958 a brand new fleet of diesel units had been ordered, the first of which entering traffic on steam train timings in late 1959. An object lesson in how to get things done! *Online Transport Archive*

A down express, headed by Stanier 'Jubilee' 4-6-0 No.45594 *Bhopal*, bursts out of Elstree tunnel and into daylight once again. The locomotive is in presentably clean condition and the smoke being emitted enhances the photograph. The train is travelling on the fast lines and the other tunnel mouth visible in the shot is used by traffic on the slow lines. The quadruple track section between St Pancras and Glendon South Junction was for many years the longest stretch of unbroken quadruple track in Great Britain. *Colour-Rail*

The Midland Railway commenced operations to Moorgate from 13th July 1868 and the link prospered for many years, so much so that on one day in 1903 7,018 passengers were recorded. This was probably the heyday of the service, however, because the development of the Underground network coupled with the growth of tram routes eroded patronage of the direct Midland service to the City. After the First World War, services ran in peak hours only and in 1930 only 20 trains a day were entering Moorgate from the former Midland line, and by 1959 this had shrunk to a mere two daily services in each direction, one to St Albans City while the other served Harpenden. In this illustration Fowler-designed Class 3MT 2-6-2T No.40024 is depicted at Moorgate some time in the late-1950s, presumably prior to working one of the evening peak-hour trains mentioned above. *RCTS Photo Archive*

A train for Welwyn Garden City, with a respectably clean Class N2 0-6-2T No.69523 in charge, waits to leave Moorgate on 30th July 1958. This locomotive was built by the North British Locomotive Co., entered service in February 1921 and was fitted with condensing apparatus for working over the Metropolitan Widened Lines from King's Cross to Moorgate. No.69523 was withdrawn in July 1962 but was subsequently saved for preservation and is the sole remaining representative of its class. Moorgate is a large station which, at the time of this picture, had two Inner Circle platforms, two electrified bay platforms and three non-electrified bays for steam-hauled services to the Midland and Great Northern (GN) lines along the Widened Lines. Connections to and from King's Cross main line station were built in the 1860s and consisted of two single line tunnels, the East Branch from the up side of the main line and Hotel Curve which gave access to the down side. *R.C.Riley*

Sir Nigel Gresley's record breaking Class A4 Pacific No.60022 *Mallard* enters King's Cross station in late afternoon sunshine with a train from the north in August 1959; the train has just emerged from Gasworks tunnel which is lost in deep shadow. Appropriately, the part of the train's formation that is visible is also of Gresley design while King's Cross station's signal box is on the right of the shot. The Great Northern Railway had obtained powers on 26th June 1846 to build its main line from Doncaster to London and after Potters Bar the line descends continuously for eight miles, involving the passage of seven tunnels. The final obstacle was the spur of high ground just north of King's Cross, this being pierced by two tunnels on a 1 in 107 gradient. A temporary passenger station was brought into use at Maiden Lane (now York Way) on 7th August 1850 and the short extension to King's Cross was ready in 1852, the first train to depart being the 7.00am 'parliamentary' to York on 14th October. Lewis Cubitt's station was plain and functional, the facade especially so, and architects commented on its low cost but GNR shareholders protested at 'the extravagance in erecting so splendid a station'. *Online Transport Archive*

The driver of Class A4 'Pacific' No.60010 *Dominion of Canada* is in classic pose as he waits to leave King's Cross with a train to Leeds in March 1963. Steam traction was officially banished from the southern end of the GN main line when King's Cross shed was closed to steam in June 1963 and No.60010 was moved to Peterborough together with other members of its class. *Dominion of Canada*'s sojourn there was brief, however, and in early November it was one of five Eastern Region Class A4s transferred to the Scottish Region where the class was enjoying an Indian summer on the recently accelerated Glasgow to Aberdeen service. It survived in Scotland until May 1965 when it was withdrawn for preservation in Canada. *Online Transport Archive*

Once described as an 'echoing vault', King's Cross was a magnet for railway aficionados and the excitement of visiting train spotters was always heightened when an A4's corridor tender suddenly emerged from Gasworks tunnel. That was an instant giveaway which identified a 'Streak' and perhaps one just ex-works from Doncaster not usually seen in London which could be underlined in spotters' ABC books. When this picture of Class A1 Pacific No.60127 *Wilson Worsdell* leaving King's Cross was taken in June 1957 the ECML's express services were entirely steam-worked apart from occasional appearances by the prototype 'Deltic'. Carmine and cream was the dominant livery for coaching stock and No.60127's rake is entirely made up of vehicles in those colours apart from the fifth vehicle which seems to be a Gresley-designed buffet car in maroon, a colour that became increasingly common as carmine and cream was phased out. Note the Class N2 0-6-2T on the left, locomotives of that class being a very familiar sight here on suburban and empty stock trains at the time. Part of the old York Road station is visible together with the East Branch which provided a valuable link for Moorgate commuters via the Widened Lines. While the lines to and from Moorgate were officially taken out of use from 8th November 1976 the platform at York Road continued to deal with a small number of terminating passenger trains until March 1977. *Colour-Rail*

Two immaculately turned out Gresley Pacifics feature in this shot of King's Cross which is thought to have been taken in the late 1950s. Class A3 No.60110 *Robert the Devil* is clearly visible while Class A4 No.60021 *Wild Swan* is partially concealed by the building. Judging by the amount of coal in No.60110's tender it was backing down into the station to take out a long-distance train. One of Thompson's rather unsuccessful Class L1 2-6-4Ts, No.67783, is also in the shot; those engines could be found on both suburban and empty stock duties in the King's Cross area. Note the 'No Smoking' sign on the end of the building in the foreground which presumably didn't apply to steam locomotives! *Colour-Rail*

The 1 in 107 climb away from King's Cross is probably the most arduous gradient faced by enginemen on the East Coast Main Line (ECML) between London and Edinburgh and in this picture Gresley Class A3 Pacific No.60061 *Pretty Polly* is seen hard at work as it leaves Gasworks tunnel with a down express in May 1963. Despite being pictured just a few weeks before the cessation of steam along the southern section of the ECML south of Peterborough, a high standard of cleanliness was still being maintained and *Pretty Polly* is in quite sparkling condition. Note the distinctive Thompson-designed coach immediately behind the locomotive, identified by its oval shaped toilet window. No.60061 entered traffic in April 1925 and escaped withdrawal until it was taken out of service in September 1963, only four months after this portrait was taken. It doesn't look like a locomotive ready for the scrapheap, does it? *Rail Photoprints*

The approach to King's Cross, as it was in the early 1960s before rationalisation of the tracks and electrification. In this photograph Class A4 Pacific No.60030 *Golden Fleece* is seen coming downhill past Belle Isle signal box (visible above the second coach) towards Gasworks tunnel with an unidentified express train on 18th March 1961. Apart from Ebonite's chimney, the shot is dominated by the substantial bridge that carries the North London line across the layout at this point while the tracks serving King's Cross goods yard and locomotive shed are immediately in front of the other signal box on the left of the picture. Behind that signal box are the goods only tracks that provided a connection from the ECML to the North London line. One wonders whether the signalmen at Belle Isle were paid a premium rate as an inducement to work at such a gloomy, noisy and very often smoky location. *R.C.Riley*

An up Newcastle train, headed by Gresley Class A4 Pacific No.60021 *Wild Swan*, passes the extensive carriage sidings and maintenance depot just north of Wood Green (later Alexandra Palace) station on 19th July 1961. The Hertford loop line, which rejoins the ECML just north of Stevenage, veers off sharply to the right while the flyover for down trains is just visible on the extreme left of the picture. At the time of this picture BR retained masses of coaches for seasonal use and, in addition, trains arriving at King's Cross would often be taken out to the carriage sidings for servicing and this may account for the huge number of carriages visible. The depot boasted a carriage washing machine, visible in the middle of the picture, and also a grounded coach body which doubtless served as a welcome refuge for shunting staff. The Wood Green area was also served by another station called Palace Gates which was on a former Great Eastern branch from Seven Sisters, but this was shut from 7th January 1963, a rare example of a BR line in the London area being closed.
Martin Smith

Class A1 Pacific No.60126 *Sir Vincent Raven* gets into its stride at the head of an unidentified northbound express near New Barnet in June 1963. The fireman appears to have been using his shovel just before reaching this location, the resultant smoke effect no doubt pleasing the photographer, and this splendid action shot resulted.
Martin Smith

The 4.12pm King's Cross to Grimsby/Cleethorpes train is seen just north of Potters Bar station with BR Standard 'Britannia' Pacific No.70028 *Royal Star* in charge on 24th September 1962. In the 1960 summer timetable this train left London at 4.15pm and was booked to arrive in Cleethorpes at 8.23pm; at that time two through King's Cross to Cleethorpes services in each direction were provided on weekdays. They were routed via the erstwhile East Lincolnshire line and served Spalding, Boston and Louth, all of which lost their London trains when the route was largely closed in October 1970, the last mentioned location being completely erased from the railway map. A batch of 'Britannia' Pacifics was based at Immingham shed to work the King's Cross to Grimsby/Cleethorpes expresses and the first representative to arrive on Humberside was No.70039 *Sir Christopher Wren* which appeared on 7th December 1960, becoming the first Pacific to be allocated to that depot. *Martin Smith*

Royal Star is seen again near Potters Bar, this time in June 1963, working an unidentified up extra train; note the first five carriages at least are of Thompson design. Records reveal that by October 1962 three 'Britannias' were allocated to Immingham and that figure had risen to seven by the following February, the locomotives involved being Nos.70035 to 70041. *Martin Smith*

Constructed between 1936 and 1944, the prodigious haulage capacity of Sir Nigel Gresley's Class V2 2-6-2s ensured that traffic along the East Coast Main Line was kept moving during difficult wartime conditions and they have sometimes been described as 'the engines that helped win the war'. Here an unidentified member of the class hauling a down express is seen approaching the end of the long 1 in 200 climb from Wood Green near Potters Bar in June 1963. Apart from the rear vehicle the train is made up entirely of Gresley- and Thompson-designed carriages, including an articulated pair of Gresley compartment coaches immediately behind the locomotive. *Martin Smith*

On 5th October 1963 the Midland & Great Northern Joint Society organised a rail tour titled the 'Wandering 1500' from London's Broad Street station which was routed over various branch lines in Northamptonshire and Warwickshire. Motive power was provided by the last surviving inside cylinder Class B12/3 4-6-0 No.61572 and in this picture this locomotive is seen laying a magnificent smokescreen across the countryside near Hatfield as it heads northwards on the first leg of the journey. This iconic locomotive was built by Beyer Peacock and out-shopped in August 1928 but was based on a much earlier Great Eastern Railway design originally introduced in 1911; No.61572 was later rebuilt with a larger boiler by Gresley. By the date of this picture it had already been officially withdrawn from BR service for two years but had been purchased by the society who were, no doubt, absolutely delighted to be given permission to use it on their special train. The enjoyment of the participants was no doubt heightened by the special's ingenious itinerary which took in the closed Bedford to Northampton line and the mainly moribund Stratford-upon-Avon & Midland Junction route from which passenger trains had been withdrawn in the early 1950s. That little-known route ran from Ravenstone Wood Junction, near Olney, to Stratford-upon-Avon via Towcester and Fenny Compton and had been retained as a goods only link. What a fascinating day out! *Martin Smith*

The Locomotive Club of Great Britain's 'North London Rail Tour' ran on 2nd September 1961 and started at Marylebone at 1.40pm with Fowler Class 3MT 2-6-2T No.40031 in charge, the destination of the tour's first leg being Moorgate. The train was routed via Wembley Stadium, Neasden, Acton Wells Junction, Richmond, Kentish Town and King's Cross Metropolitan and locomotives were changed on arrival at Moorgate. The train is seen here at Harlesden Midland, between Brent and Acton Wells Junctions. Unfortunately, the lettering on the train's home made headboard is not clearly visible but this is unlikely to have worried the participants, some of whom were probably hard pressed to name some of the more obscure junctions over which they passed. *John Millbank*

The 'North London Rail Tour' is seen again, this time at East Finchley with Gresley Class N2 0-6-2T No.69568 at its head, the N2 having replaced No.40031 at Moorgate. Following departure from Moorgate the train was routed via King's Cross Metropolitan and Finsbury Park and continued to High Barnet on the Northern Line. The Class N2 later powered the train from High Barnet to Dalston East Junction where former Midland Railway Class 3F 0-6-0T No.47202 took over for the last stage of the tour via Lea Bridge and South Tottenham to St Pancras where the train arrived at 7.35pm. *John Millbank*

A repeat performance. Interest in the LCGB's 'Great Eastern Suburban' rail tour was such that the first train, run on 7th April 1962, was over subscribed and a second tour had to be hastily arranged: this ran three weeks later on 28th April. The second train was advertised as the 'Great Eastern Suburban Rail Tour No.2' and Class N7 0-6-2T No.69621, which also hauled the first train (illustrated elsewhere in this album) took the participants on the initial stage of the journey from Liverpool Street along the branch to Palace Gates, a popular destination among enthusiasts because closure of this North London backwater was rumoured. The next part of the journey took the passengers through the complex series of junctions at Temple Mills and on to Chingford, terminus of another Great Eastern Railway branch which by that date was served only by suburban electric units, and no doubt the arrival of the steam train created quite a stir. A change of motive power took place at Chingford with the Class N7 locomotive being replaced by Class J15 0-6-0 No.65476, and this machine hauled the train through the maze of lines at Stratford and then along London Transport's tracks to Ongar, then the easternmost outpost of the Central Line. Later the veteran Class J15 took the train down to North Woolwich and eventually returned the participants to Liverpool Street after, no doubt, a very rewarding tour. The history of the J15s can be traced back as far as 1883 but No.65476 arrived much later on the scene having entered traffic in August 1913. *David Wigley*

Authorised by the North London Railway (NLR) Act of 22nd July 1861, Broad Street station opened on 1st November 1865 and originally the premises consisted of seven platforms and a substantial adjacent goods yard, the latter being opened a little later, in 1868. The station frontage was quite impressive, being 250ft long and 110ft high with a clock tower as its centrepiece. Another platform was added in 1891 and in 1913 a further platform was constructed giving a total of nine, so it was quite a large station though somewhat overshadowed by the more prominent, main line Liverpool Street station next door. Remarkably, at one time Broad Street was the third busiest London terminal with 27 million passengers being recorded in 1902 and in 1910 the LNWR introduced a long-distance service to Birmingham and Wolverhampton, but this was abruptly curtailed in 1915 by the First World War. Broad Street station and the NLR probably reached their zenith in about 1900 and thereafter both suffered a catastrophic decline as the tramway and Underground networks spread. The goods yard closed in January 1969 while later the same year four platforms were taken out of use and the inevitable occurred on 30th June 1986 when the doors were closed for the last time. Here, Stanier Class 5MT No.44774 poses near Broad Street's signal box in the early 1960s when the station was still served by a couple of rush-hour steam workings from Tring. *Colour-Rail*

A rare colour view of steam traction inside Broad Street station on 27th April 1958. The train depicted is the RCTS 'Hertfordshire Rail Tour No.2', the first major stop being at Harrow & Wealdstone where participants changed onto another set of coaches before being treated to a trip along the branch to Stanmore hauled by Stanier Class 2P 0-4-4T No.41901. The branch was still open for passenger traffic as far as Belmont at that time while the remaining section to Stanmore, which closed to passengers in September 1952, remained open for goods traffic. Later in the day the train visited the Watford to St Albans Abbey line and continued along the goods only section to Hatfield. The final leg of the trip took passengers back to central London via Hertford North, the tour finishing at Broad Street as depicted here. One of the locomotives rostered for the tour, Class N7 No.69614, failed in the early stages of the journey and classmate No.69632 substituted. *Online Transport Archive*

On 4th July 1836 the Eastern Counties Railway (ECR) was authorised to build a line from London to Norwich and Yarmouth and the first section from Bethnal Green to Romford opened on 20th June 1839. The route to Norwich was progressively opened in stages and that city was reached in 1849; meanwhile a westward extension from Bethnal Green to to Shoreditch (later Bishopsgate) was brought into use on 1st July 1840. A separate company opened a line from Stratford, where it connected with the ECR, to Cambridge in 1845. The terminus at Bishopsgate was inconveniently sited and was quickly becoming inadequate to deal with the amount of traffic on offer and in December 1863 it was announced that a new terminus was to be constructed at Liverpool Street, and this opened for suburban traffic on 2nd February 1874. Soot encrusted buildings provide a drab background to this illustration of BR Standard 'Britannia' Pacific No.70037 *Hereward the Wake* simmering at the Liverpool Street locomotive servicing point in the early 1960s; another 'Britannia' is largely concealed behind No.70037. A water crane and brazier are visible and there was also a turntable, coal supply (note the wagon) and an inspection pit. A cab road was conveniently positioned behind the installation and offered a grandstand view of operations but the author recalls that spotters had to have their wits about them because some of the taxi drivers clearly did not, and hurried down the slope at breakneck speed, anxious to pick up their next customer. A young man can be seen peering over the parapet in an attempt to identify the locomotives and while *Hereward the Wake* probably presented little difficulty, the engine nearer to the slope was, perhaps, more of a challenge. *Rail Photoprints*

3rd · SINGLE	SINGLE · 3rd
LIVERPOOL STREET (M) TO	
Liverpool Street (M)	Liverpool Street (M)
DOWNHAM	DOWNHAM
DOWNHAM	
via Littleport	
For alternative routes see book of routes	
(E) 12/9	Fare 12/9 (E)
For conditions see over	For conditions see over

9394 9394

Train spotters positioned on the cab road at Liverpool Street had the bonus of being able to spot locomotive movements on the adjacent line into Broad Street station which was in an elevated position. That terminus was basically a suburban station, most services being formed of electric units (EMUs) to and from Richmond while a rush hours-only service to Watford Junction, also formed of EMUs, was only marginally more exciting. It is recorded that one or two rush hour workings to Tring remained steam worked in the early 1960s and the 6.05pm departure was observed with steam traction in the summer of 1962, so occasionally the spotters had something to cheer about. In this shot a Birmingham Railway Carriage & Wagon Type 2 Bo-Bo can be seen on the Broad Street line as 'Britannia' Class 4-6-2 No.70006 *Robert Burns* awaits its next turn of duty at Liverpool Street. *Rail Photoprints*

All that jazz. Liverpool Street station's smoke-blackened surroundings are in stark contrast to the absolutely outstanding condition of Class J69 0-6-0T No.68619 which was engaged on station pilot duty in the autumn of 1958. Clearly a favourite at Stratford shed, in 1959 No.68619 was repainted in GER blue livery and earmarked for Liverpool Street station pilot duty where it must have gained many admirers. This dainty machine was a member of a class originally introduced in 1902 for suburban passenger work in the London area and this particular example was out-shopped from Stratford works in May 1904. In the early 1920s the GER was faced with severe overcrowding on its trains from Liverpool Street to Chingford/Enfield and introduced five-coach articulated sets known as 'Quint-Arts' together with a more frequent timetable, probably the most intensive steam service ever operated in Great Britain. The class of accommodation on the new stock was denoted by a colour code at door top level, prompting the nickname 'Jazz Trains'. Remarkably, the diminutive class J69 locomotives bore the brunt of these workings for a brief period until the more powerful N7s came into use. *Ken Wightman*

Inevitably, perhaps, the BR Standard 'Britannia' Pacifics were the most photographed steam locomotives at Liverpool Street and this appealing portrait of No.70034 *Thomas Hardy* completes a trio of shots of those machines. This was the first of the BR Standard classes, appearing in January 1951 when No.70000 *Britannia* was released from Crewe works. *Rail Photoprints*

The last months of steam at Liverpool Street. The cavernous, smoke-filled station may not have been particularly welcoming to ordinary passengers in the early 1960s but at least it had plenty of atmosphere, although whether this was appreciated by the travelling pubic is open to question. Here, in this picture taken in June 1962 just three months before steam bowed out, smoke drifts lazily from the chimney of Class N7 0-6-2T No.69725 as it awaits its next duty. Barrows loaded with parcels provide the perfect obstacle course for unwary passengers while on the left a gleaming Brush Type 2 A1A-A1A diesel locomotive represents the new age of the railway. Once a regular sight on suburban trains, a mere nine Class N7 locomotives lasted into 1962, from a class that once numbered 134 engines, and those were included in the final cull of steam motive power that occurred at Stratford in September 1962. *Online Transport Archive*

1st-SINGLE   SINGLE-1st

6930

6930

Sudbury (Suffolk) to

Sudbury (Suffd'k)
London
(Liverpool Street)

Sudbury (Suffolk)
London
(Liverpool Street)

LONDON (LIVERPOOL STREET)
via Marks Tey

(E)   24/0   Fare   24/0   (E)
For conditions see over   For conditions see over

The exemplary condition of its locomotives was a hallmark of Stratford shed and in this picture a smartly turned out Class B1 4-6-0 No.61311 is seen at the head of an unidentified departure on 14th May 1957. The B1s were one of the few steam locomotive classes equipped with electric train identification lights and No.61311 is also displaying white headcode discs which were essential to enable signalmen to identify the train during daylight hours. On the right is one of the 1,500 volt dc four-car electric units built in the late-1950s for use on the Liverpool Street to Southend Victoria service. This part of Liverpool Street station, known as the east side, was opened in April 1894 and consisted of eight platforms. The approach to Liverpool Street from Bethnal Green, descending at 1 in 70 through a deep and gloomy cutting, originally consisted of four tracks but was increased to six in 1891. Incredible though it may seem, Bishopsgate Low Level station (closed 22nd May 1916) was located in this smoke-filled cavern and joining or leaving trains there must have been quite an experience. *R.C.Riley*

The 12.33pm Liverpool Street to Clacton and Walton-on-Naze train ascends the 1 in 70 Bethnal Green bank behind 'Sandringham' Class B17/6 4-6-0 No.61656 *Leeds United* on 28th February 1959. The bulk of the locomotives of this class were constructed at Darlington works, but outside contractors were also used, the first ten machines being built by the North British Locomotive Co. while the last eleven to be built were constructed by Robert Stephenson & Hawthorns Ltd. No.61656 was a Darlington works-built example, entering traffic in May 1936 and surviving until 1960 during which year the last engines of the class were taken out of service. The first 48 locomotives were named after country houses, the class taking its name from No.61600 *Sandringham* the first member of the class, while the remaining 25 locomotives were named after football teams but some name changes later occurred. *R.C.Riley*

Passengers were left in no doubt regarding the destination of this train and would certainly have no grounds for complaint if they boarded the wrong train. Here, in this portrait which was taken on the same day as the previous shot, one of Stratford shed's spotless stud of Class N7 locomotives is seen at Bethnal Green. For many years Stratford apparently had 492 locomotives on its books the largest allocation of any shed in Great Britain though it should be mentioned that many engines were sub-shedded at a variety of suburban depots. When the depot closed to steam traction on 8th September 1962 there were fewer than 50 locomotives allocated. Stratford shed marked the end of steam by specially cleaning three Class B1 4-6-0s which were lined up for photography and one of those, No.61156, subsequently powered a relief Harwich Parkeston Quay to London relief train which was reportedly the final BR steam working on the GE main line. Steam was officially banned at Liverpool Street from 10th September and such workings ceased south of March from the same date. Truly the end of an era when the familiar, rhythmic beat of a Westinghouse brake pump would no longer echo around Liverpool Street station. *R.C.Riley*

A Cambridge express has just breasted the bank from Liverpool Street and passes through Bethnal Green station on the bright autumn day of 7th October 1958. The locomotive is Class B2 No.61607 *Blickling* which was originally built by the North British Locomotive Co. in December 1928 as a three cylinder Class B17 but was one of ten locomotives rebuilt by Thompson with two cylinders and a '100A' Class B1 type boiler. 1958 was *Blickling*'s last full year in traffic, it being withdrawn from service in December 1959 and broken-up during the following month. Unbelievably, electrification of the heavily used suburban routes into Liverpool Street was mooted way back in 1905 however the GER, and later the LNER, baulked at the idea due to the heavy expenditure involved but in 1935 improvements were agreed with the Treasury which supported capital works to relieve unemployment. The outbreak of hostilities in 1939 badly delayed the programme and ten years elapsed before 1,500 volts d.c. electric trains started running to Shenfield and one of the original units is just visible on the left of the shot. Electrification of the Enfield/Chingford routes via Hackney Downs was not completed until 1960 but this at least enabled steam photographers to take pictures unobstructed by overhead masts and wiring, as seen here. *R.C.Riley*

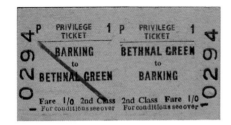

An express from Norwich to Liverpool Street nears the end of its journey and passes through Stratford some time in the late 1950s. The locomotive at the head of the train is BR Standard 'Britannia' No.70002 *Geoffrey Chaucer* which provides positive proof that not quite all locomotives on the GE line were maintained in exemplary condition. Note the train's formation which includes BR Standard, Gresley and Thompson-designed vehicles. *Ken Wightman*

The 2¼ miles-long line from Seven Sisters to Palace Gates was opened as far as Noel Park on 1st January 1878 and throughout on 7th October. Palace Gates was laid out as a through station for it was intended to continue over the GNR main line to an end-on junction with the Muswell Hill Railway at Alexandra Palace, but nothing came of this plan. Palace Gates eventually became a through station for goods and occasional passenger workings in 1929 when the LNER laid a connection with the Hertford loop line. Latterly, the passenger service was restricted to rush hours only supplemented by a few Saturday lunchtime trains but there was no Sunday service. The 1960 Eastern Region summer timetable lists around half a dozen trains from Palace Gates during the morning with a similar number of return services in the evening, all of which ran to or from North Woolwich. Palace Gates was close to Wood Green station (later Alexandra Palace), the latter being much more convenient for commuters, so perhaps it came as no surprise when passenger services were withdrawn from 7th January 1963 and the line was subsequently dismantled. Here, Thompson Class L1 2-6-4T No.67730 is seen at the intermediate station of West Green with a train to Palace Gates in June 1962. *Online Transport Archive*

When the branch was constructed clearly no expense was spared in providing a very substantial footbridge at Palace Gates – perhaps the promoters were hoping to cash in on the popularity of the nearby Alexandra Palace and anticipated huge crowds. However, when this picture was taken in September 1962 the writing was already on the wall for the branch and weeds were taking hold on the platforms. In this portrait Class N7 0-6-2T No.69621 is seen simmering in the station after arrival with a train from North Woolwich in September 1962 shortly before the elimination of steam traction from the Great Eastern section in the London area. *Online Transport Archive*

A further view of Palace Gates station, this time showing Thompson Class L1 tank locomotive No.67729 standing at the up platform after arrival with an evening train, also in September 1962. Except for No.67701, the first engine to be constructed, all of these locomotives were built in the BR era, the class numbering 100 examples which were built by BR at Darlington, the North British Locomotive Company and Robert Stephenson & Hawthorns Ltd. No.67701 appeared in 1945 as the prototype and almost three years elapsed before No.67702 emerged from Darlington works in early 1948. The final locomotive constructed was No.67800, this entered traffic in September 1950 and the class lasted until December 1962 when the last example was withdrawn. *Online Transport Archive*

The line from Stratford (Low Level) to North Woolwich was opened by a local company to Canning Town on 29th April 1846 and throughout on 14th June 1847. When the Royal Victoria Dock was opened the line was diverted onto the north side of the new dock with the old line on the south side becoming the Silvertown Tramway. When the Royal Albert Dock was opened in 1880 the line was diverted again, this time into a tunnel beneath the waterway and the original line became part of the dock railway. In 1870 a large gas works was constructed at Beckton and the Great Eastern Railway (GER) ran a passenger service for workmen to and from Stratford commencing on 17th March 1874, and remnants of this survived until December 1940. The GER took over operation of all passenger services on the North Woolwich line in 1896 and at the turn of the century there was a very intensive service of 50 passenger trains each way daily plus many goods workings. In this picture Class N7 0-6-2T No.69724 poses at Stratford (Low Level) with a train to North Woolwich on 11th April 1961. *Rail Photoprints*

The Stratford to North Woolwich
line may have been barren territory
for lineside photographers but at
least a road overbridge just west
of North Woolwich station gave an
uninterrupted view of the station
premises. Here, Class N7 No.69640
is seen leaving with the 1.40pm to
Stratford (Low Level) on 24th June
1961. The quite commodious station
possessed all the paraphernalia of a
small terminus, including a goods yard,
signal box, semaphore signals and
a substantially built water tank. The
handsome station building, partially
visible on the right, is a gem, brick
built with stone trimmings in Italianate
style and an attractive balustrade at
the front. When the Eastern Counties
Railway opened the line in 1847 to
link with their ferry across the river
Thames they cheekily called the
station 'North Woolwich' with the aim
of enticing passengers travelling to
that part of south-east London, and
those passengers may have been a
trifle surprised to find they had to cross
the river to reach Woolwich proper.
R.C.Riley

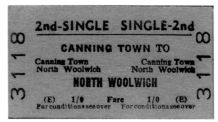

The Great Eastern Railway operated
a very frequent steam suburban
service to and from Liverpool Street
so perhaps it was entirely appropriate
that the nearby Stratford to North
Woolwich line went down in history
as the last intensively worked steam
route in the capital. During peak hours
there was a train every 15 minutes,
so from the photographers' point of
view the route's drab surroundings
were compensated by the frequency
of the service. Photographed on the
same day as the previous shot, Class
N7 No.69670 is seen entering North
Woolwich station with the 1.38pm
ex-Stratford. The towering cranes of the
King George V Dock are visible on the
right and they provide a reminder that
it was the development of Royal Docks
that brought prosperity to the line.
R.C.Riley

A sprightly old timer. In this really vintage scene Class 1P 0-4-4T No.58062 is depicted near Ockendon with a three coach train from Upminster to Grays in 1955. Despite its dreadful external condition the locomotive is bustling along in the sunshine. No.58062 was one of a total of 205 0-4-4Ts designed by Samuel Johnson for the Midland Railway and constructed in three separate batches with considerable design differences. The locomotive seen here was one of the final series built between 1889 and 1900 with 5ft 4in diameter wheels and higher boiler pressure than their predecessors; they were also marginally more powerful. No.58062 was constructed by Dubs & Co. and entered traffic in February 1892, and when this shot was taken it was in its last full year of service, being withdrawn in February 1956. Five locomotives of this class were allocated to Plaistow shed in 1953, presumably for use on this service, but the class was quite widely distributed and perhaps the machines with the highest profile could be found on the Somerset and Dorset line. There they worked the Highbridge branch until the arrival of Ivatt 2-6-2Ts and the last survivor was No.58086 which was withdrawn from Bath (Green Park) shed in July 1960, though it had reportedly been out of use since May 1959. *Rail Photoprints*

In the 1830s steamers on the river Thames were booming and it was said that the Gravesend ferry alone was carrying a million passengers a year. Most steamers called at Brunswick Wharf, Blackwall, and in 1836 a line from Minories to Blackwall was proposed by the Commercial Railway. Three years later that company changed its name to the London & Blackwall Railway when the short extension to Fenchurch Street was authorised, the station opening to passenger traffic in August 1841. A link with the Eastern Counties Railway, via Bow Junction, opened on 2nd April 1849, with regular through services being inaugurated in 1854. Meanwhile, the North London Railway commenced operating to Fenchurch Street during 1850 but, perhaps, the most significant development occurred a few years later in 1858 when London, Tilbury & Southend Railway (LTSR) trains started running to Fenchurch Street via Gas Factory Junction at Bow. The LTSR was in a parlous state for many years but the appointment of a new, energetic general manager in 1875 brought about a dramatic change in the line's fortunes as substantial passenger traffic to and from Southend was developed. On 1st June 1888 a cut-off was brought into use from Barking to Pitsea, avoiding Tilbury, and the considerable reduction in journey times ensured a further boost to passenger traffic and resulted in a vastly increased frequency of the train service. This is Stanier 2-6-4T No.42528 at Fenchurch Street on 9th August 1961. *Colour-Rail*

Barking is a major traffic centre on the LTSR route offering interchange facilities with two Underground lines and the connection across north London to Gospel Oak. In this early 1960s picture an Underground train waits in the adjacent platform as Stanier Class 4MT 2-6-4T No.42501, in very respectable condition, runs in with a lengthy eastbound train. This locomotive design was a development of the Fowler 2-6-4Ts which appeared in 1927, the first of the Stanier locomotives being a small batch (Nos.42500 to 42536) designed especially for the LTSR section and fitted with three cylinders unlike the bulk of the class which only had two cylinders. *Colour-Rail*

A morning train from the Kent coast arrives at Cannon Street station behind Bulleid 'West Country' Pacific No.34004 *Yeovil* in October 1958; *Yeovil* worked one of the last steam trains from that station on 12th June 1959. Commuters from the north Kent coast were reasonably well catered for and in 1957 all five of the weekday early morning trains were booked to run to Cannon Street, but all the later services ran to Victoria. A city terminus adjacent to Cannon Street was authorized on 28th June 1861 and opened on 1st September 1866, not long after the opening of neighbouring Charing Cross in January 1864. The next major chapter in the history of Cannon Street occurred in 1926 when the station's rather cramped nine platforms were rebuilt to form eight faces and an enlarged circulating area was created. Despite its lowly status as principally a commuter station, Cannon Street boasted prominent towers that jutted out across the north bank of the river Thames, providing one of the capital's most striking landmarks. The arched roof suffered wartime damage and was removed in the late-1950s. *Rail Photoprints*

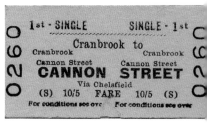

On the Southern Region's South Eastern Section the crack train of the day in the 1950s was the 'Golden Arrow' from Victoria to Dover Marine, and Stewarts Lane shed ensured that a highly polished locomotive was rostered. In the summer 1957 timetable 'The Arrow', as it was known colloquially, left Victoria at 2.00pm and was routed via Folkestone, the arrival time in Paris being 9.41pm. In the reverse direction the train left Paris at 12.24pm and was routed via Dover Marine, the advertised arrival time in London being 7.30pm. This arrangement would certainly have suited the motive power department, the trains being worked by one locomotive which, presumably, reversed at Dover Priory before joining the return working. In this illustration the 'Golden Arrow' is seen near Petts Wood with the customary gleaming Pacific in charge, in this case No.34091 *Weymouth*; this shot is believed to date from the late 1950s. *Ken Wightman*

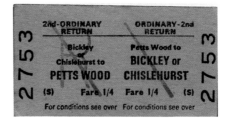

Opposite below: A view across London's ever changing skyline towards Charing Cross, apparently taken from a high vantage point offered by the roof of Waterloo station. An unidentified express, doubtless destined for the Kent coast, is getting under way behind a Bulleid 'West Country' Pacific while a Class H 0-4-4T waits on an adjacent track with empty stock for a later long-distance departure. The approach road to Waterloo station is visible in the foreground. London Bridge station was on the fringe of central London, and the South Eastern Railway (SER) needed a terminus closer to the centre and a scheme to extend across the river Thames by a high level route was approved by Parliament in August 1859. The approach to Charing Cross is across Hungerford Bridge which is clearly visible in the picture; originally the bridge carried only four tracks but was widened to accommodate six, albeit at the expense of one of the public footpaths across the river. Charing Cross station opened, as previously mentioned, in January 1864; suburban trains used the station from 11th January while main line services commenced at the beginning of May. A curious feature of the layout at the approach to Charing Cross is the erstwhile connection from a siding which was projected across Waterloo's concourse to join the SER's tracks. The purpose of this is not immediately clear and it was removed when Waterloo station was rebuilt in the 1920s, but the stub is visible, presumably in use as a locomotive refuge road, and traces of a platform were still to be seen many years later. *Rail Photoprints*

One of the few lines in the London area to lose its passenger service was the 4¾ miles-long branch from Dunton Green to Westerham. The South Eastern Railway obtained parliamentary authority to build a branch from Dunton Green but the powers lapsed, much to the dismay of local landowners and traders in the Westerham area who had been agitating for a link with the expanding rail network. Eventually a local company was formed to construct a line and later the SER agreed to manage, maintain and operate the branch which opened for passenger traffic on 7th July 1881. There was one intermediate station at Brasted, Chevening Halt being added in 1906. The line was optimistically built for double track but it remained single throughout its life. The branch suffered due to Westerham's close proximity to Oxted station from where more convenient, direct London services run to both London Bridge and Victoria and declining receipts in the 1950s led to the withdrawal of Monday to Friday off peak trains so the branch was reduced in status to 'rush hours only'. A full service continued to operate at week-ends but there were long gaps in the timetable and the service closed rather early, the last Saturday train from Westerham in the 1957 summer timetable being at 7.23pm. The writing was clearly on the wall and the Southern Region's decision to close the line could hardly have come as a shock to the local populace. Here, Class H 0-4-4T No.31551, emblazoned with the Union flag and bearing chalk inscriptions, is depicted at Dunton Green with one of the final workings on 28th October 1961 as three local lads look on, no doubt puzzled by all the fuss. The tracks of the main line from London to Tonbridge and Dunton Green's signal box are visible. The very last trains were formed of seven carriages with main line locomotives at each end so the line went out in style. There was strong support for a preservation scheme but this was regrettably thwarted by government plans for a road scheme and the intrusive M25 motorway now runs where the 'Westerham Flyer' once chugged sedately along. *Tim Stephens*

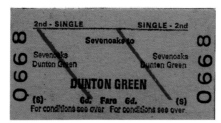

The London, Brighton & South Coast Railway's (LBSCR) first west end terminus was south of the river Thames at Pimlico and this came into use on 29th March 1858. On 23rd July of the same year the Victoria Station & Pimlico Company was incorporated to construct a short extension from the West End & Crystal Palace Railway, at what is today Stewarts Lane Junction, across the river Thames on Grosvenor Bridge to a new terminus at Victoria on the site of Grosvenor Canal Basin. The 'Brighton' subscribed half of the capital and when the new station opened on 1st October 1860 it was entitled to half of the premises, with the remainder being leased to the London Chatham & Dover Railway (LCDR). The latter used temporary premises until its own station was ready on 25th August 1862. The two halves of the station were always known as the 'Brighton' side and the 'Chatham' side. Two major developments on the 'Brighton' route were the construction of a cut off from Croydon to Balham Junction, opened in 1862, and a high level line from Pouparts Junction (east of Clapham Junction) to the south end of Grosvenor Bridge which opened on 1st December 1867. The LCDR gained easier access to Victoria when it opened a route from Penge Junction, west of Beckenham, to Stewarts Lane in August 1862 and a continuation on another high level line to Grosvenor Bridge which came into operation in January 1867. Remarkably, the Great Western Railway had a foothold in the LCDR side of Victoria running a service from Southall inaugurated on 1st April 1863; this ceased from 22nd March 1915. The frontage of the two stations was unimpressive and in 1898 the LBSCR obtained an Act authorizing rebuilding of their side of the premises, this being formally opened on 1st July 1908. During the following year the SECR, which had succeeded the LCDR, completed its new, but much plainer, station building in Portland stone which features an arch inscribed 'The Gateway to the Continent'. The Southern Railway (SR) knocked a wide opening in the wall dividing the stations in 1924 and unified administration, but the two halves of Victoria continued to have duplicated passenger facilities for many years afterwards. Victoria is the most cosmopolitan of the London termini and in the post war era commuters, continental travellers, day trippers and racegoers mingled on its concourses, not to mention visiting Heads of State for whom the red carpet was rolled out. This picture was taken on the former LCDR 'Chatham' side of the station and shows Bulleid 'Battle of Britain' Class Pacific No.34074 *46 Squadron* getting under way with an unidentified passenger working some time in the late 1950s. The headcode indicates a Dover-bound train via the Chatham route but that might be misleading because it was not unknown for firemen to forget to change headcode discs or even display the wrong route indication. No.34074 was one of the first of its class to be withdrawn in June 1963 and has been said to have been the most camera shy of all Bulleid's light Pacifics. *Rail Photoprints*

A helping hand. Smartly turned out Class H 0-4-4T No.31551 provides energetic rear-end assistance to the lengthy 11.00am boat train from Victoria, the train engine of which is already out of sight round the curve; this picture is thought to have been taken in the mid-1950s. Note the train's formation which includes Bulleid and Maunsell-designed coaches plus a Pullman car in distinctive umber and cream livery just visible towards the front. In the 1957 summer timetable the 11.00am departure ran via the Dover to Calais cross channel route, the arrival time at the French port being 2.20pm. First class passengers had the advantage of a fast onward train to Paris Nord where the advertised arrival time was 6.10pm but second class travellers had to rely on a slightly later and considerably slower train from Calais which arrived in the French capital at 6.40pm. *Rail Photoprints*

Stewarts Lane shed was responsible for providing motive power for the annual Derby Day special conveying HM the Queen from Victoria to Tattenham Corner and in 1962 one of the locomotives diagrammed as a stand-by was Maunsell 'Schools' 4-4-0 No.30901 *Winchester* which is depicted at the depot on 8th June 1962 in sparkling condition. The special was actually worked by sister locomotive No.30926 *Repton* while other reserve motive power, which was stationed at various strategic locations to assist in the event of a failure, included Billinton Class K 'Moguls' Nos. 32343 and 32353. A 4-SUB electric unit can be seen on the South Western main line into Waterloo while the four towering chimneys of Battersea power station provide an unmistakable backdrop. Sadly, just over six months after this portrait was taken *Winchester* and the two 'Moguls' were victims of a savage cull of 'Southern' steam power in order to reduce the number of locomotives inherited by the newly created British Railways Board. *Rail Photoprints*

An occupational hazard of authors of railway albums is the unfortunate fact that in steam days some locations were widely photographed while others were hardly visited by railway photographers. The immediate area of Shortlands is definitely in the former category primarily because the late Ken Wightman lived in a property that backed on to the line and reportedly a gate at the bottom of his garden gave him instant access to the lineside. On one occasion he was on hand to record the embarrassing scene of the failed electrically-hauled 'Golden Arrow' being pushed into Shortlands station by a following electric train – not the kind of image that would have won a BR poster competition. In this scene no such problem appears to be affecting Class L 4-4-0 No.31775 as it steams past Downsbridge Road bridge with a Ramsgate 'extra' on 3rd August 1957. Introduced in 1914 by the SECR, this class numbered 22 examples, twelve of which were constructed by Beyer Peacock while the remainder were built by A. Borsig in Berlin, this being one of the very rare occasions when a British railway company awarded a contract to an overseas builder. Fortunately, the locomotives' components arrived in Great Britain just before the start of the First World War and their erection was supervised by Borsig's fitters at Ashford. No.31775 proved to be a wise investment and gave 45 years' service before being withdrawn in August 1959. *Ken Wightman*

Travelling in style. The well-to-do clientele patronising the prestigious 'Golden Arrow' probably took trunks and large suitcases away with them, hence the large bogie van at the front of the train, after all it wouldn't do to take heavy luggage into a Pullman car that might obstruct a waiter while he was serving the minestrone soup. Here, Bulleid 'Merchant Navy' Class Pacific No.35028 *Clan Line*, in the customary immaculate condition, heads past Downsbridge Road bridge on its way to the coast in September 1958. A trio of 'Merchant Navy' Pacifics - the others were Nos. 35001 *Channel Packet* and 35015 *Rotterdam Lloyd* – was based at Stewarts Lane shed for the most arduous Eastern Section passenger assignments. *Rail Photoprints*

In the late 1950s much of the route between Victoria and the north Kent coast resembled a building site as work was underway for the forthcoming electrification. A major part of the expenditure was focused on improving the track layout at various locations in order to speed-up services which were slow compared to other parts of the system. On the right of this photograph a huge pile of earth has been excavated from the side of the cutting in order to lay two more tracks at the approach to Shortlands station, doubtless with a view to eliminating conflicting train movements. An up boat train, hauled by Bulleid 'Merchant Navy' Pacific No.35001 *Channel Packet*, is passing but the locomotive was in scruffy condition and presumably not in favour for working the 'Golden Arrow' at that time, for which an impeccable standard of cleanliness was mandatory. At least its train is colourful with a priceless collection of liveries before the dreaded words 'corporate livery' entered the vernacular. This picture was taken in October 1957. *Rail Photoprints*

Complete with all the usual regalia, Bulleid 'Battle of Britain' Pacific No.34088 *213 Squadron* seems to have the task of hauling the 'Golden Arrow' well in hand as it passes Downsbridge Road bridge. No.34088 was rebuilt in April 1960 and steam traction powered the 'Golden Arrow' for the last time on 11th June 1961, so the picture must have been taken during that period. *213 Squadron* finished its career in absolutely appalling condition on the South Western Division in March 1967. The 'Golden Arrow' left Victoria in the mid-morning during the mid-1960s, the precise departure time being determined by the summer and winter time used in Great Britain, and arrived in Paris at 5.50pm. The single second class fare from London to Paris via Dover/Calais in 1964 was £5.4s.0d. (£5.20p.). *Ken Wightman*

In stark contrast to today's monotonously predictable railway scene, there was much variety of motive power to be observed at Shortlands especially during the summer months when many seaside day excursions from the Midlands ran to the Kent coast with 'foreign' locomotives. Inevitably, perhaps, many trains originating on the London Midland Region were worked by Stanier Class 5MT 4-6-0s and here No.44716 is seen at the head of a down Ramsgate excursion conveying a trainload of passengers doubtless eagerly anticipating a few hours on the beach before the trek back to the station for the return journey home. *Ken Wightman*

Bulleid 'Merchant Navy' Pacific No.35028 *Clan Line* takes a down boat train from Victoria to Folkestone Harbour through Bromley South on 23rd June 1957. The formation comprises a remarkable selection of rolling stock in a variety of liveries, including crimson and cream, green, and umber and cream while the train engine sports Brunswick green, albeit rather faded. When this shot was taken modernisation was still some way off and Bromley South remained semaphore signalled, a signal box being visible in the middle of the picture. The goods yard, on the left of the photograph, remained very much in business and was accessed from the main line by a track that appears to cross the entire layout. *Clan Line* was one of the last 'Merchant Navy' Class engines to be built, in December 1948, and was the final member of the class to be rebuilt, in November 1959, and this machine survived the cutter's torch and remains active on the main line at the time of writing. *Rail Photoprints*

Unashamed luxury. Between 1911 and 1924 the London Brighton and South Coast Railway (LBSCR) built a large number of coaches for its overhead a.c. suburban services, nearly all of which were converted to d.c. when the a.c. operation was abandoned in the late-1920s. When this stock was withdrawn in the early 1950s some vehicles were deemed to be in reasonable condition and were formed into 18 four-car units which were intended as a stopgap until replacements were delivered. In the event the units were forced to soldier on until 1960 by which time they were thoroughly worn out. Part of one of those vintage units is visible on the right of this shot as Bulleid 'West Country' Pacific No.34091 *Weymouth* charges through Bickley with the down 'Golden Arrow' in July 1955. One wonders what went through the minds of the luckless suburban commuters herded aboard their ancient, draughty and rattling train as they caught a glimpse of the pampered passengers on the 'Arrow' sitting in the sumptuous comfort of their cosy armchairs as afternoon tea was being served. 'I say, waiter, I wouldn't mind another plateful of those fondant fancies'. *Rail Photoprints*

London Bridge, opened in 1836 by the London & Greenwich Railway, is the capital's oldest terminal station and, like Victoria, originally consisted of two separate stations side-by-side. In 1839 the London & Croydon Railway opened an adjacent station and from 1841 shared its tracks with the London & Brighton Railway. The SER arrived on the scene in 1842, but the various companies were unable to reach agreement on enlarging the premises and in 1863 the LBSCR, formed by the amalgamation of the 'Brighton' and 'Croydon' companies, built its own premises and the SER also constructed a station for its sole use. The LBSCR's arched train shed was acclaimed for its style and economy and the Terminus hotel was built alongside its station, but that was a financial failure and was later bought by the 'Brighton' company who converted it into offices. In 1864 the SER built five high level through platforms and undertook further work in 1893, and by 1902 there was a total of 21 platforms. The Southern Railway united the two halves of the station in 1928 but London Bridge was still a confusing place, this being aggravated by the destruction during the Second World War of much of the frontage and adjacent former hotel. In the 1970s BR undertook a major reconstruction scheme which swept away what remained of the old buildings but the overall roof on the former 'Brighton' side was retained. In this panoramic picture, which appears to have been taken from the signal box, Class E4 No.32463 is depicted in the former LBSCR part of the station with a short van train on 14th May 1959. The inevitable suburban electric unit occupies the adjacent platform while platform barrows, so long a common sight at British railway stations, can also be seen. The magnificent overall roof was London Bridge station's redeeming feature but this, alas, had to be sacrificed when a further extensive rebuilding was undertaken as part of the Thameslink improvement scheme. *R.C.Riley*

The layout of London Bridge station must have baffled passengers who did not use the station regularly and one of its curiosities was the bank of four rather cramped platforms sandwiched between the 'Brighton' side terminal platforms and 'South Eastern' through lines which were on a higher level. The four platforms were apparently a late addition and built on the site of a tiny goods depot that was closed in 1899. Here, on 8th April 1963, a rather scruffy Class E4 0-6-2T No.32474 is seen in platform No.10, somewhat dwarfed by the footbridge and high level through platforms on the right. This part of the station was gloomy and desperately in need of a lick of paint as all of the installations look dilapidated. No.32474 was withdrawn from traffic in December 1962 and consigned to a dump of redundant locomotives in Hove goods yard. The early part of 1963 was bitterly cold, however, and Brighton shed was desperately short of motive power, a situation that was exacerbated by an accident involving sister engine No.32468 which was immediately withdrawn. In mid-January No.32474 was salvaged from the dump and returned to traffic at Three Bridges shed where it was put to use on East Grinstead passenger trains. It later found further employment at Norwood Junction shed on local duties but its reprieve could not last forever and on 11th May it was despatched to Eastleigh works for breaking-up. *David Clark*

The Railway Correspondence & Travel Society (RCTS) was formed in Cheltenham and for many years a drawing of Maunsell 'Schools' Class locomotive No.30925 *Cheltenham* was used as their logo, featuring on many of their publications. During the autumn of 1962 rumours were rife that a major reduction in the BR steam fleet was planned prior to the formation of the British Railways Board which succeeded the British Transport Commission in January 1963. When the RCTS was planning a rail tour to Sussex *Cheltenham* seemed a natural choice of motive power for the first stage of the trip from London Bridge to Brighton and here it is depicted climbing Forest Hill bank in the south London suburbs on 7th October 1962, a misty autumn day. A platform diversion at the start caused the train to be slightly late passing Bricklayers Arms junction with the result that the bottom of Forest Hill bank was passed at only 38mph. Later on the journey the 'Schools' locomotive reached a much more creditable 75mph at Copyhold Junction at the approach to Haywards Heath. After a trip down the Seaford branch behind a couple of venerable 'Brighton' tank engines the participants returned from Brighton to the capital via Steyning behind Billinton Class K 'Mogul' No.32353. *Martin Smith*

Opposite: The history of Bricklayer's Arms shed can be traced back as far as 1844 when it was opened by the South Eastern Railway (SER) and it became the largest on its system, responsible for numerous goods turns and passenger workings from Charing Cross and Cannon Street. At the turn of the 19th century the shed had an allocation of 150 locomotives but despite having a larger allocation Bricklayers Arms was seen as secondary in importance to Stewarts Lane when the SER amalgamated with the London Chatham & Dover Railway. 'The Brick', as Bricklayers Arms was known to railwaymen, benefited from a series of improvements, including a new repair shop, reconstruction of the 'old' shed plus a water softener and larger turntable were installed. The depot was badly damaged during World War II and that period marked the start of a decline in its fortunes, modernisation schemes in the 1950s causing a dramatic fall in steam duties. The shed closed its doors in 1962 by which time there were a mere handful of turns for its surviving allocation of Maunsell 'Moguls' and Bulleid Pacifics. The depot consisted of a number of separate buildings and occupied a substantial site, and here Wainwright Class C 0-6-0 No.31271 is seen on 2nd January 1962 in the company of Class N 'Mogul' No.31867. *Rail Photoprints*

Designed for transfer goods work, the undistinguished Maunsell Class W 2-6-4Ts never had a high profile and probably rank as one of the least photographed 'Southern' steam classes. The first five locomotives were built in 1932 at Eastleigh and the remaining ten at Ashford in 1935/36. These machines had three cylinders, weighed 90 tons 14 cwt. and had a tractive effort of 29,450lb. In the early 1950s the entire class was based in the London area, principally at Hither Green and Norwood Junction sheds, but some ended their days in Devon on banking duties between Exeter St David's and Central where they replaced the Class Z 0-8-0Ts. No.31917 was photographed at Norwood Junction shed in September 1962; the last examples were taken out of traffic in August 1964. *Rail Photoprints*

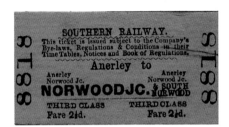

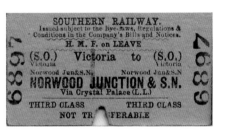

A Maunsell 3-set represents a very modest load for BR Standard 2-6-4T No.80081 as it heads away from Clapham Junction with a Victoria to Tunbridge Wells West train on 10th September 1961. Built at Brighton, No.80081 entered traffic in April 1954 and spent much of its life on the LMR at Bletchley for working commuter trains to London. In about 1959 it was transferred to the Southern Region where it lasted until withdrawn in June 1965. *R.C.Riley*

The hot, dry summer of 1959 was responsible for many fires on railway embankments and cuttings as evidenced here by the burnt grass visible in this shot of Fairburn Class 4MT 2-6-4T No.42106 leaving Clapham Junction on 20th June with the 4.08pm Victoria to Tunbridge Wells West train. The formation comprises a Maunsell 3-set plus a loose Maunsell SK (Second Corridor) vehicle immediately behind the locomotive. No.42106 was a Brighton-built locomotive but when this scene was recorded No.42106's career on the 'Southern' was coming to an end because in December 1959 the entire SR allocation of 34 Fairburn 2-6-4Ts was exchanged for a similar number of BR Standard engines from the LMR. The newcomers included No.80081 which is depicted in the previous shot. *R.C.Riley*

BR Standard 2-6-4T No.80081 is seen again, this time leaving East Croydon on a train to Tunbridge Wells West on an unknown date in the early 1960s. Clearly, the photographer's principal aim was to record the passage of the steam train whose days were numbered but during the ensuing years virtually everything visible in this picture has disappeared. The station has been totally rebuilt, a new road bridge has been constructed alongside that seen here, the residential property has been demolished and the track layout changed beyond recognition to reduce conflicting movements. Perhaps the only feature that survives today is the cutting wall and also, unbelievably, the remains of the a.c. electrification steelwork, the position of which is indicated by the small areas of concrete just visible at the top of the wall above the second and fourth coaches. Who would have guessed it? *Colour-Rail*

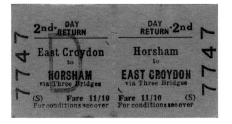

The surrender of steam on the Oxted line. The first diesel units were drafted on to Oxted line diagrams in June 1962 and steam workings were progressively reduced as further units came on stream. In May 1963 some diesel locomotive turns were introduced, using machines made redundant by freight train economies on the South Eastern Division, and these made further inroads to those steam duties that remained. On 29th June No.34013 powered the 7.17am Brighton to London Bridge train, this reportedly being the last rostered appearance of a Bulleid Pacific on the Oxted line. Another blow was the closure of Tunbridge Wells West shed as an independent depot on 9th September but at least basic servicing facilities were maintained for a little longer. In this portrait BR Standard 2-6-4T No.80010 is seen passing through South Croydon with an evening London-bound passenger working. *John Millbank*

A Victoria to Brighton train via Eridge is seen near Sanderstead on 23rd June 1961 with Maunsell 'Schools' Class 4-4-0 No.30936 *Cranleigh* in charge. The train is made up of two distinctive sets of coaching stock, the leading 4-coach set being of Maunsell design while at the rear is a Bulleid 3-coach set. No.30936 may not appear in this shot to be making much effort but the six miles-long climb from South Croydon to Woldingham, much of it at 1 in 100, was really hard work for steam locomotives and their crew. *Rail Photoprints*

The London & South Western Railway's (LSWR) first London terminus was at Nine Elms but in 1848 it opened a new terminus near Waterloo Bridge. That was a ramshackle affair with a mere four platforms under a wooden roof and during the rest of that century it was extended piecemeal as traffic developed. By 1885 there was a jumble of 16 platforms and four areas that could be regarded as concourses, and to add to the confusion a track crossed the central concourse on the level, passed through the front wall and crossed Waterloo Road on a bridge to join the SER's Charing Cross line. A most peculiar addition, known as the 'Cemetery Station', was made in about 1853 by the Necropolis & National Mausoleum Company which operated a regular service of trains for coffins and mourners to Brookwood cemetery. The LSWR vowed to radically improve Waterloo, and between 1900 and 1922 it was entirely rebuilt with 21 platforms and a spacious, single concourse beneath a vast roof. The station was totally transformed from one of the worst termini to one of the finest and, indeed, with the entire complex covering 24½ acres it ranked among the largest and busiest in Great Britain. The frontage is particularly fine, incorporating the company's offices and an impressive victory arch of Portland stone forming a memorial to staff lost in two world wars. Waterloo will be forever etched on the memories of railway aficionados because it became the last London terminal station to be served by regular steam workings, the final sevice into Waterloo being the 2.07pm from Weymouth on 9th July 1967. In this rare colour view of the station's interior, photographed on 10th June 1965, the driver of BR Standard 4-6-0 No.73092 can be seen oiling round in time-honoured fashion after arrival at Platform 10 with an express from Bournemouth. This locomotive was actually in lined Brunswick green livery but its paintwork is hidden by a liberal coating of grime. Note the poster welcoming people to Britain – at that time Cunard liners still crossed the Atlantic and B.O.A.C was a company flying to all corners of the world. *Roy Denison*

Many photographs of Bulleid Pacifics waiting to leave Waterloo have been taken over the years, no doubt encouraged by an uncluttered background of canopies and the vast expanse of the station roof which added interest. Here, No.34007 *Wadebridge* is pictured standing at the head of a train to Bournemouth West in the mid-1960s; the locomotive is still displaying its nameplates and shield. This machine attained just over 20 years in service, being built at Brighton in September 1945 and surviving in traffic until October 1965. *Tim Stephens*

During 1965/66 the main line from Waterloo to Bournemouth was bedevilled by mile after mile of engineering works as engineers struggled to relay track and prepare for electrification while at the same time the operators were actually trying to run a train service. During the spring of 1967, with the inauguration of electrification imminent, many speed restrictions were lifted and this enabled the more enthusiastic crews to 'have a go' with steam. There are numerous reports of Bulleid Pacifics 'doing the ton' during the last weeks of steam operation, thus ensuring that steam traction went out on a high note. In this portrait, Bulleid Pacific No.34060 *25 Squadron* is depicted apparently waiting to leave Waterloo with a 'Union Castle Express' boat train but in reality it was working the 6.54pm to Salisbury on 30th June. Perhaps the headboard had been affixed by one of the shed staff at Nine Elms with a sense of humour, after all the end of steam was only a few days away and nobody would have objected to a bit of fun, would they? *Roy Denison*

When steam traction was in its prime it would have been unthinkable for a dirty locomotive to be diagrammed to haul the 'Bournemouth Belle' but when this shot was taken in June 1966 it was known that steam's days were numbered and standards were slipping, as exemplified here by the dreadful condition of No.35008 *Orient Line*. The grimy locomotive at least has its number and nameplates still *in situ* but nobody has bothered to affix a headboard. The 'Belle', as it was universally known to railwaymen, offered the last word in luxury and elegance and, of course, meals were served at every seat by stewards in Pullman uniform. The 'Bournemouth Belle' made its debut with limited operation in July 1931 but from January 1936 it operated on a daily basis, usually with a Maunsell 'Lord Nelson' 4-6-0 as motive power. The train ceased running during the Second World War and when it resumed it was usually powered by an air-smoothed Bulleid Pacific hauling a train of immaculate Pullman cars which must have created a real impression on people at a time when rationing and fuel shortages were still prevalent. Steam haulage of the 'Belle' officially came to an end in January 1967 when the duty was handed over to Brush Type 4 diesel locomotives but in practice steam traction made frequent appearances such as on 5th July 1967, during the last week of steam, when No.34024 *Tamar Valley* hauled the down train while sister engine No.34036 *Westward Ho* took the up service. Perhaps if BR had been really enterprising they could have retained a small stud of steam locomotives in smart condition for use on the stylish 'Belle' and advertised the train's undoubted attractions. After all, it was in a class of its own. *Rail Photoprints*

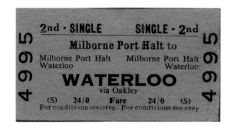

Towards the end of its life Nine Elms shed was characterised by dust, dereliction and decay but it will always be remembered as London's last steam shed. There was an engine shed on the site from the earliest days of railways, probably dating back to 1848 when the extension was completed to Waterloo. The first part of the modern depot, as steam enthusiasts will remember it, was a 15 road, brick building with a pitched, slated roof which was erected in 1889. In 1910 an eleven road extension was authorised alongside the existing shed and two years later a 65 ft turntable was installed. The two sheds stood side by side and, not surprisingly, were known as the 'old' and 'new' sheds. The next substantial landmark in the history of Nine Elms shed concerns the construction of a massive 400 ton ferro concrete coaling plant which was authorised by the LSWR but did not come into operation until 1923, by which time the Southern Railway had been formed. The construction of a water softener and installation of an engine washing plant in 1936 were the only improvements carried out by the 'Southern' and enemy bombing during the Second World War inflicted severe damage, particularly to the shed roof. Repairs were effected in asbestos after the war but some sections of the old shed's roof were never replaced, surprising perhaps in view of the depot's status as the most important on the South Western Section. The BR era also saw little attempt to modernise the shed: perhaps there was no incentive because the shed's allocation was being steadily reduced from 100 engines in the late 1950s to a paltry 25 at closure in July 1967. Towards the end basic tools such as oil feeders, buckets and hand brushes would be in frustratingly short supply and crews resorted to hiding equipment in case it 'disappeared'. Despite the generally filthy and dilapidated state of the shed premises Nine Elms cast its spell over many enthusiasts and inspired film makers and photographers, in particular the world renowned artist, the late David Shepherd, who brilliantly captured the unique atmosphere of the place. In this picture, taken on 2nd June 1967, two BR Standard Class 5MTs stand forlorn among the ruins of the depot surrounded by piles of ash and general debris. The 'new' shed is on the right of the photograph while the building in the background, in the middle of the picture, is a surviving remnant of the 'old' shed. The girders in the foreground at one time formed part of the entrance to the 'old' shed. *Roy Denison*

A remarkable development in late 1958 was the allocation of Western Region pannier tank locomotive No.9770 to Nine Elms shed for use on empty stock workings between Waterloo and Clapham Yard. Eleven more Class 8750 locomotives were transferred to the Southern Region in January 1959 with a view to ousting the elderly Drummond Class M7s at Nine Elms and Dover shed's Class R1 0-6-0Ts used for banking between Folkestone harbour and Folkestone Junction. The pannier tank locomotives, which were built in the 1940s, were quite modern machines compared to the Class M7s, a design that dated from 1897. On 24th March, however, No.9770 was despatched to the West Country for trials on the Padstow to Wadebridge/Bodmin service with the intention of replacing the Class O2s on that route; it later returned to the London area. Further transfers of Class 8750 locomotives were made later in 1959. The performance of the Class 8750 locomotives based at Dover came in for some criticism when it was discovered that the WR had sent engines overdue for shops and No.4601 had reportedly run 201,295 miles since its last general overhaul. Here, No.4634 is seen rounding the curve at the approach to Vauxhall station on 20th June 1959 with a long train of empty coaches destined for Waterloo. It should be noted that Class 8750 locomotives were also based at Southern Region sheds in the West Country. *R.C.Riley*

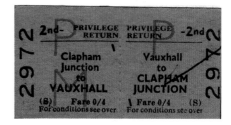

The distinctive overhead signal box provides an instant clue to the location of this photograph: yes, it is Clapham Junction. Drummond Class M7 0-4-4T No.30249 represents the 'old order' on empty stock workings between Clapham Junction and Waterloo; this picture was taken in October 1958 just before the influx of pannier tank locomotives from the Western Region. The detailed history of this unremarkable locomotive is not known but it was certainly on the books at Nine Elms in the early 1950s and it is possible it spent much of its working life on the dreary 'day in, day out' task of shuttling between those points. No.30249 entered service in May 1897 and remained in traffic until July 1963. *Rail Photoprints*

Bulleid 'West Country' Pacific No.34032 *Camelford* heads westwards through Clapham cutting with an unidentified train in September 1965; the locomotive is in clean condition and complete with nameplates. The slow lines, that are used by suburban services, are on the right of the picture. The Southern Railway formed many of its locomotive-hauled coaches in fixed set formations and the number on the end of the leading vehicle indicates that it was formed in Set No.786 which consisted of three carriages. *Rail Photoprints*

Government approval for the electrification of the Bournemouth line was given in the autumn of 1964 and the announcement set a date for the elimination of steam traction on the Southern Region (SR). This prompted an immediate surge in the number of enthusiasts' rail tours and societies vied with each other to produce the most ingenious itinerary or spectacular motive power. The Locomotive Club of Great Britain (LCGB) clearly had friends in the BR hierarchy and arranged for one of the Scottish Region's (ScR) last remaining Gresley Class V2 2-6-2s to make the long journey south to work a special on the SR on 3rd July 1966. The locomotive selected was No.60919 of Dundee shed but this machine was in delicate condition and failed at Nine Elms shed with a broken spring on the morning of the tour so Bulleid Pacific No.34002 *Salisbury* had to be hastily substituted; it is seen here just after passing Clapham Junction. The SR operating authorities really entered into the spirit of the occasion and, following a quick repair, they arranged for No.60919 to run down to Bournemouth where it was hoped it would be able to haul the tour over its final stage. Alas, when it reached Eastleigh an injector fault was diagnosed and it was decided it would be too risky to let No.60919 loose on the special train, so it was sent 'light engine' to Basingstoke where it suffered yet another defect. *Rail Photoprints*

Even in the best regulated industries accidents can sometimes happen and BR maintained a fleet of breakdown cranes at various major engine sheds to deal with incidents. In this picture a colourful crane, together with its associated tool and riding vans, is seen heading south near Clapham Junction on 16th June 1967 with a rather unkempt BR Standard Class 3MT 2-6-2T No.82029 in charge. Breakdown cranes were normally observed simmering in light steam 'on shed' so the photographer was very fortunate to see one out on the line and, of course, be in a good position for a photograph. This picture was taken during the final few weeks of steam operation on the Bournemouth line and it is recorded that, most unusually, No.82029 powered the 7.18am Waterloo to Salisbury train on Saturday 8th July during the last weekend of steam working. This was No.82029's final journey in steam and on arrival at Salisbury it retired to the dump of withdrawn locomotives on Salisbury shed. *Martin Smith*

The sun may not have been shining but the photographer was no doubt delighted when he took this picture of Maunsell 'King Arthur' Class 4-6-0 No.30798 *Sir Hectimere* passing through Clapham cutting with the 2.54pm Waterloo to Basingstoke train on 23rd April 1962. This once numerous class was down to eight representatives by that date and No.30798 was in its last few weeks of use, being withdrawn in June. It had been built at Eastleigh and was out-shopped in June 1926, so had given good service. The last surviving 'King Arthur' was No.30770 *Sir Prianius* which was taken out of traffic in November 1962. A BR Standard Full Brake vehicle (coded BG in railwayman's parlance) is formed immediately behind the locomotive while those coaches that are visible are of Bulleid design. The local lines are on the right of the shot. *R.C.Riley*

The gentleman standing on the adjacent platform appears to be transfixed as gleaming Maunsell 'Lord Nelson' Class 4-6-0 No.30851 *Sir Francis Drake* speeds through Raynes Park station on 25th August 1957. The headcode suggests it was working a Waterloo to Bournemouth West train. The first example of that class built was No.30850 *Lord Nelson* which entered traffic in August 1926 and a further 15 locomotives followed in the 1928-29 period; the last members of the class were withdrawn from service in October 1962. Considered by some experts to be the most handsome 4-6-0s ever to run in Great Britain, for a short period in the 1920s the 'Lord Nelsons' were the most powerful locomotives running in the country but lost that status when the GWR introduced the 'Kings'. The locomotive is hauling a distinctive rake of five Bulleid carriages with the bodyside panelling extended over the solebars, indicating the vehicles normally ran as a six-car Bournemouth dining set which had that distinguishing feature. *Rail Photoprints*

In the 1930s the Southern Railway under Sir Herbert Walker undertook a massive programme of electrification and created the 'Southern Electric' image to promote the company. Several stations were reconstructed with straight lines and the green and black décor that was fashionable at the time, and one of the most striking was Surbiton in the south-west London suburbs which was built in 1937. The style was not well received by some critics at the time, however, being dubbed unkindly 'Odeon cinema style' or even more disparagingly as 'super wireless sets' but more enlightened observers have subsequently acknowledged Surbiton station's claim to fame as one of the first to 'acknowledge the existence of a modern style'. Regrettably, the trains seen in this photograph taken on 19th August 1966 hardly enhance their impressive and elegant surroundings. Grimy Bulleid 'West Country' Pacific No.34047 *Callington* is passing through on an up train comprised a hotchpotch of vans and multi-coloured coaches while the electric unit on the slow line is one of the notoriously uncomfortable 2-HAL units, many of which had bench type seats and painted compartment interiors. Note the two train spotters sitting in the sunshine on the down platform. *Martin Smith*

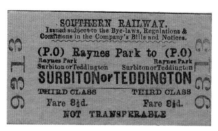
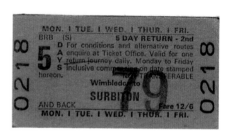

A splendid, panoramic view of Feltham marshalling yard with part of the motive power depot in the foreground; this picture was taken looking westwards in 1958. Among the locomotives in evidence are representatives of the two very powerful LSWR tank classes introduced by Urie in 1921 shortly before the Southern Railway came into being. The machine nearest to the camera is No.30520, one of five Class H16 locomotives designed for heavy goods duties, while the adjacent engine is No.30495, a member of the G16 Class specially built for hump shunting at Feltham. Two very grimy Class Q1 0-6-0s are stabled nearby while most of the other engines in the picture are 350hp diesel shunting locomotives. Feltham was overwhelmingly a freight shed, this being reflected in its allocation in the late 1950s including no fewer than 25 Class S15 4-6-0s, more than half the class, which powered goods trains across the South Western Section. The shed consisted of six through roads plus a small repair shop located at the eastern end. A hump is visible in the middle of the picture whilst in the background the vast expanse of the marshalling yard stretches almost as far as the eye can see. *Rail Photoprints*

The Willesden (West London Junction) to Clapham Junction line was opened on a piecemeal basis, the first section southwards from Willesden to Kensington being opened by the West London Railway on 27th May 1844. The mixed gauge, single track line was 2½ miles long but traffic was very sparse, the line traversing an area that was open country at the time. Initially, the route crossed the GWR on the level at Wormwood Scrubs but in 1860 the crossing was replaced by a bridge and three years later the route had a change of fortune when the West London Extension was opened to Clapham Junction on 2nd March 1863. This stretch was mixed gauge, double track and the West London Railway doubled their section at about the same time, thus providing a double track route throughout. Connections were laid with the GWR, while at the southern end direct running on to the Chatham and Brighton lines was possible and the line quickly assumed much greater importance, particularly for through transfer freight. Kensington station was rebuilt in 1869 in LNWR style and given the suffix 'Addison Road'. Passenger traffic never attained large proportions despite some innovative ideas, such as the GWR's Southall to Victoria service which ran from 1863 to 22nd March 1915, and the LNWR's Broad Street to Kensington service which was later extended to Victoria. The Underground and buses offered much more direct routes to the West End and City, and between the wars passenger usage was on a downward spiral, the Second World War hastening the demise of the few remaining services which were withdrawn altogether in 1940. After the end of hostilities holiday trains from the north and various special workings appeared and, of course, the route continued to carry substantial tonnages of goods traffic. The general growth in passenger traffic throughout the London area, and the capital's crippling road traffic congestion, has led to the development of the West London line for suburban and some moderately long distance travel, and another change of fortune so the line is probably busier today than at any time in its history. In this view of Kensington (Olympia) station a couple of Class B1 4-6-0s, No.61063 (on the left) and No.61183 prepare to leave with northbound holiday trains on 18th August 1956. *R.C.Riley*

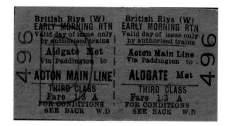
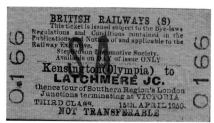

This scene may, at first sight, appear to be just another inter-regional holiday train heading towards Willesden, where the locomotive would give way to LMR electric traction. In fact this shot is far from being another everyday scene because it was taken on Saturday 8th July 1967, the penultimate day of BR steam traction in the entire London area, and shows a Portsmouth Harbour to Colne special passing Kensington (Olympia) station on the down through line. *Martin Smith*

Kensington (Olympia), BR's forgotten backwater. During the 1960s Kensington (Olympia) was probably best known as the starting point for many long-distance BR car-carrying services which were marketed as 'Motorail' and in 1967 the network offered trains to such far-flung destinations as Holyhead, Penzance and Perth. A shuttle service was provided from Earls Court by London Transport when events were scheduled at the adjacent exhibition centre while goods and seasonal passenger trains continued to use the through lines but there was no regular, advertised local passenger service. In the mid-1960s Kensington (Olympia) was not listed in the Southern Region (SR) public timetable while it merited only a brief mention in the London Midland Region version. There was, however, a regular, unadvertised passenger service for Post Office workers to and from Clapham Junction and this 'secret' service was steam hauled until steam traction was banished from the SR in July 1967. In this picture BR Standard Class 3MT 2-6-2T No.82029 is seen gingerly exiting from Kensington on 20th August 1965. *John Millbank*

Ivatt 2-6-2T No.41298 awaits departure from Kensington (Olympia) with a train to Clapham Junction on 26th May 1967. The coach formed immediately behind the locomotive is the experimental glass fibre compartment vehicle, No.S1000. Both the locomotive and coach have been preserved. *Rail Photoprints*